Integrative Theraplay® Approach for Children on the Autism Spectrum

Also in this series

Parenting with Theraplay®
Understanding Attachment and How to Nurture a Closer Relationship with Your Child
Vivien Norris and Helen Rodwell
Illustrations by Miranda Smith
Forewords by Phyllis Booth and Dafna Lender
ISBN 978 1 78592 209 1
eISBN 978 1 78450 489 2

Theraplay®—The Practitioner's Guide
Vivien Norris and Dafna Lender
Foreword by Phyllis Booth
ISBN 978 1 78592 210 7
eISBN 978 1 78450 488 5

Theraplay®—Theory, Applications and Implementation
Edited by Sandra Lindaman and Rana Hong
Foreword by Phyllis Booth
ISBN 978 1 78775 070 8
eISBN 978 1 78775 071 5

Theraplay®—Innovations and Integration
Edited by Rana Hong and A. Rand Coleman
Foreword by Phyllis Booth
ISBN 978 1 78775 591 8
eISBN 978 1 78775 592 5

Integrative Theraplay® Approach for Children on the Autism Spectrum

Practical Guidelines for Professionals

A. Rand Coleman and **Rana Hong**

Foreword by **Dr. Richard Allen**

Jessica Kingsley Publishers
London and Philadelphia

First published in Great Britain in 2024 by Jessica Kingsley Publishers
An imprint of John Murray Press

2

A CIP catalogue record for this title is available from the British Library and the Library of Congress

ISBN 978 1 78775 068 5
eISBN 978 1 78775 069 2

Printed and bound in Great Britain by CPI Group

Jessica Kingsley Publishers' policy is to use papers that are natural, renewable and recyclable
products and made from wood grown in sustainable forests. The logging and manufacturing
processes are expected to conform to the environmental regulations of the country of origin.

Jessica Kingsley Publishers
Carmelite House
50 Victoria Embankment
London EC4Y 0DZ

www.jkp.com

John Murray Press
Part of Hodder & Stoughton Limited
An Hachette UK Company

Contents

Foreword

As of 2022, the rate of autism in children was 1 out of 48. As this ratio has significantly increased over the last 20 years, many scientific strides have been made to help better identify and support individuals on the autism spectrum in the home, school, and community settings. The most predominant, effective, and evidence-based interventions for these individuals are based on the principles of Applied Behavior Analysis (ABA) (National Autism Center 2015). Indeed, many manualized intervention approaches include common evidence-based instructions derived from ABA, such as prompting, reinforcement, chaining, and shaping (NPDC n.d.).

A more recent critique of autism intervention approaches within the field of ABA itself has focused on ensuring these include critical components such as social validity, quality of life, generalization of skills, and a focus not just on skill acquisition but also on overall compassion and emotional wellbeing for children on the autism spectrum and their families. For example, contemporary behavior analysts have advocated for focusing on ensuring learners are in a positive mood, relaxed state, and highly engaged during learning (e.g., Iovino *et al.* 2022), and focus on positive interactions and support with the learner during the pairing process between therapist and learner (Schramm & Miller 2014). Recent literature reviews on effective autism intervention have also highlighted the positive impact of naturalistic developmental behavioral interventions (NDBIs) (Sandbank *et al.* 2020). NDBIs focus on strategies based on the principles of ABA to teach skills from a developmental sequence, and focus on using positive natural consequences (Schreibman *et al.* 2015). There is an emphasis on reciprocal interactions between children with caregivers and therapists during play activities (Sandbank *et al.* 2020).

Theraplay techniques are based on developmental and attachment theories to offer structured programming and activities to increase the social communication skills and other adaptive needs in children on the autism spectrum. *Integrative Theraplay Approach for Children on the Autism Spectrum* includes activities and their rationale, coupled with evidence-based instructional skills such as modeling, prompting, reinforcement, and functional behavioral assessment (FBA). This book focuses on intervention and programming targets designed to not simply increase adaptive skills but also to build positive relational experiences, social reinforcement, and shared enjoyment during interactions between children and their families.

Activities and principles of relationship in Theraplay can help propel programming toward the fundamental, yet often overlooked, core dimensions of ABA, including socially significant generalized behavior that improves the quality of life and represents a long-lasting behavior change—socially significant in that the techniques emphasize building strong attachment between children on the autism spectrum and their caregivers, promote positive interactions with the child's family and support team members, and ultimately increase the effectiveness of caregiver-mediated interventions.

This practical guide emphasizes social interaction in fun and simple ways that promote social connection and non-verbal communication. Activities are also developmentally appropriate and can be scaled up and down to match different ages and ability levels. The activities are easily modeled for caregivers, and can be transferred to many different family members, such as siblings, grandparents, aunts, and uncles. Parent training sessions are also based on evidence-based practices in ABA, including modeling, role-play, in vivo practice, corrective feedback, and shaping.

Therapists and caregivers will find this book provides great detail on Theraplay techniques and the rationale behind them. Theraplay using interactive activities will help caregivers and therapists to pair successfully with the child and support the child to acquire social communication skills and other critical adaptive skills. These skills can be maintained by generalized conditioned reinforcers such as caregiver affirmation and positive attention. As the authors astutely point out, when a collaborative relationship is developed between a child and caregiver, staff, or teacher, the relationship itself becomes the positive reinforcer for many other activities.

Dr. Richard Allen, PsyD, NCSP, BCBA-D

Acknowledgments

This book exemplifies knowledge and expertise in using Theraplay for children on the autism spectrum acquired over many years, thanks to the teachings and collaboration of our incredible mentors and colleagues. The completion of this book would not have been possible without their help and support. They include, but are certainly not limited to, the following:

Thanks to the leaders of The Theraplay Institute—Phyllis Booth, MA, LCPC, LMFT, RPT/S, and Sandra Lindaman, MA, MSW, LCSW, LISW-CP—words cannot express our gratitude and appreciation for all your contributions to Theraplay. Kay Schieffer, MA, MEd, and Mandy Jones-Fischer, MSW, JD, LCSW, RPT—thank you for your faith in us.

John Malikowski, BCBA, Erik Young, MEd, LMHC, LPC, and other Devereux Functional Assessment team members—thank you for sharing your innovative ideas about behavior therapy and for modeling compassion, genuine caring, and playfulness in the context of applying behavioral principles.

Seyoung Kim, PhD, LCSW, RPT, Hyunjung Shin, PhD, LCSW, RPT, and many colleagues from the Korean Association of Theraplay—thank you for generously sharing your innovative Theraplay activities and experiences specific to children on the autism spectrum.

A very special thank you to our editor at Jessica Kingsley Publishers, Sean Townsend—without your patience and support throughout this entire process, this book would not be complete. Numerous barriers at our end made any deadline seem impossible; thus, we thank you for your support in seeing this book through to fruition.

Lastly, our deep appreciation and gratitude to the children and families from whom we learn every day. Thank you for sharing your precious experiences with us.

The Authors

A. Rand Coleman, PhD, is a graduate of Hahnemann University Hospital, where he obtained a degree in Clinical Psychology, specializing in Neuropsychology. A Licensed Psychologist and Certified Theraplay Trainer and Supervisor, his clinical experience includes child neuropsychology, family intervention for children on the autism spectrum, supports for youth and adults with intellectual disabilities, and therapeutic approaches for youth with reactive attachment disorder, trauma, and severe behavior problems. After working for many years in residential care programs that serve youth or adults with serious developmental disabilities, Dr. Coleman now works in a group practice in Malvern, PA, conducting evaluations and providing both individual and family therapy.

Rana Hong, PhD, LCSW, RPT-S, is a Clinical Research Assistant Professor in the School of Social Work at Loyola University Chicago. She is a methodologically grounded Clinical Researcher, Educator, and Clinician who has a depth of knowledge and experience in children, adolescents, and families with issues of attachment, trauma, motion/behavioral disturbance, and neurodevelopmental disorders. While focusing on research in the areas of neurobiology, thematic analysis, metric development, and program (or intervention) evaluation, Dr. Hong holds clinical expertise with distinguished certifications. She is a Certified Theraplay® Practitioner, Supervisor, and Trainer, Certified Parent–Child Interaction Therapy® (PCIT) Therapist/Within Agency Trainer, Certified Eye Movement Desensitization and Reprocessing® (EMDR) Therapist and Consultant, and DIRFloortime® Expert Training Leader. As the past president of the board at The Theraplay Institute, Dr. Hong is dedicated to supporting Theraplay research and practice.

Contributing author

Susan Bundy-Myrow, PhD, RPT-S, is a Licensed Psychologist in private practice, Autism Consultant, Play Therapy Supervisor and Clinical Assistant Professor in the Department of Psychiatry, University at Buffalo, The State University of New York. As an Affiliate Trainer for The Theraplay Institute in Chicago, Dr. Bundy-Myrow has helped to bring Theraplay to professionals around the world, and developed a model for Multiple Family Group Theraplay for children on the autism spectrum. Together with David L. Myrow, she is a recipient of the Ann Jernberg Award (2011). She has published in the area of autism, including "Family Theraplay®: Connecting with Children on the Autism Spectrum" in L. Gallo-Lopez & L. C. Rubin (eds) *Play-Based Interventions for Children and Adolescents with Autism Spectrum Disorders* (Routledge, 2012).

Chapter 1

Introduction

 Walking up a hill across the school campus on our way to the cafeteria, 10-year-old Tyler and I (A. Rand Coleman) approached a dormitory for residential students at this specialized school for youth on the autism spectrum. About 100 yards from the dormitory, Tyler turned toward me and said emphatically, "I hate that sound! I really hate that sound!" A youth on the autism spectrum, Tyler struggled with social skills and language, so when he made a statement with such clarity and force, as his therapist, I took note.

I stopped with Tyler on the path and listened, but heard nothing unusual. "What sound do you dislike?" I asked.

Tyler pointed to a one-story ranch-style villa and said, "That sound! It is so loud." Again, it was unclear to me what the sound was, and I prompted him to clarify. He urgently pointed at a window with an air conditioner, saying, "That sound, that sound. It drives me crazy!"

"You mean the sound of the air conditioner?" I asked, to which he replied, "Yes, and the one at the cafeteria is even worse. I have to go eat there, but it makes me want to scream and hide." In a flash of clarity, I realized that we might now have an answer to some of Tyler's mysterious behaviors, specifically, screaming, hiding, flapping, and rocking furiously, occurring at random times, with no clear cause. While I could barely hear the air conditioner—and even when I did notice it, I blocked it out of my consciousness—to Tyler it might be so intense as to cause real auditory discomfort. I asked, "So that sounds really loud to you, all the way over here?" He nodded "yes." "And do the air conditioners at your house bother you?" He indicated "yes," again.

This revelation was a first step in identifying intense hypersensitivities that created a cumulative level of discomfort for Tyler every day. Sounds were intense and loud to him, certain clothing textures distracted him, and some smells were so intense as to seem almost toxic. He coped by various means, including repetitive rocking, hiding in enclosed spaces, running around a room and flapping his hands, or screaming, yelling, and stripping off clothes when pressured beyond endurance.

Autism Spectrum Disorder (ASD) affects approximately 30–60 youth per 10,000 (Rutter 2007), although more recent epidemiological research places the incidence much higher, at around 1% (Davidovitch *et al.* 2020). Actual incidence can be hard to determine due to the spectrum nature of the disorder—cutoff points and definitions may differ between research studies. Diagnostic criteria techniques have become more refined, enabling clinicians to detect autistic features with greater subtlety and at earlier ages. Researchers point out that more refined evaluation and earlier diagnosis has contributed to a dramatic rise in the number of children and youth diagnosed on the autism spectrum (Davidovitch *et al.* 2020; Rutter 2007).

The rise in diagnosed children on the autism spectrum, and the increased awareness of the problems associated with ASD, has been the impetus for developing therapeutic and educational interventions. As a developmental disability, school districts across the United States are required to provide free and appropriate education with necessary accommodations to children on the autism spectrum (Center for Autism & Related Disorders 2022), and many countries across the world have similar guidelines (van Kessel *et al.* 2019). Similarly, the rises in numbers, awareness, and need have driven the creation of many different approaches to education and therapy. Indeed, a short list of evidence-based interventions by the National Professional Development Center on Autism Spectrum Disorders (NPDC 2022) listed 27.

Table 1.1 highlights both the range of autism as well as the intellectual spectrum.

Table 1.1. Autism spectrum and intellectual spectrum

Autism spectrum	
Mild autism	Severe autism
Mild social awkwardness	Severe social deficits
Misses some social cues	Unable to read facial expressions
Tends to have very intense interests and focuses "excessively" on them	Literal interpretation of language
	Possible absence of language
Mild sensory hypersensitivity in one or two modalities	Many repetitive motor movements
	Incapacitating sensory overload
Intellectual spectrum	
Advanced intellectual skills	Severely delayed intellectual skills
Exceptional memory	Impaired reasoning
Exceptional academic skills in an area(s):	Severe academic delays globally
Math	Lack of abstraction
Chemistry	Unable to read or do math
Engineering	Absence of language
Cell biology	Limited executive skills
Logic	
Advanced language knowledge	
Good executive skills	

Tyler was a youth with borderline intellectual delays but severe autistic symptoms that interfered with his communication and social awareness. Sensory discomfort was a substantial driver of his behavioral outbursts, and difficulty expressing himself verbally added to his frustration. He struggled with verbal communication and social skills, which made it hard for him to express his wants, needs, and discomforts to caregivers, teachers, and therapists. Aggression or throwing things or running away, and strong and disruptive behavioral expressions became his method of communication. Tyler failed to comprehend the social relevance of clean clothes or brushing his teeth, resulting in low motivation for such things; nor did he appreciate the social and life skill importance of cleaning, cooking, or handwashing.

A multimodal approach to therapy was necessary for Tyler: social communication skills were a significant part of speech therapy and educational activities, while non-verbal communication, social play skills, and emotional regulation were practiced in small group programming. A structured system of teaching adaptive skills that included a motivational reward program was necessary to teach important self-care and domestic skills, and to motivate Tyler to use the skills regularly. Lack of awareness of social norms could lead to disruptive or impolite behavior in public, such as cutting in lines or calling out in movies and restaurants. Thus, a systemic program of learning community skills incorporated teaching, meaningful social fun, positive reinforcement of appropriate behaviors, and repetitive skills practice across multiple settings.

In contrast to Tyler, Sarah came to therapy as a nine-year-old due to having difficulty with peer relationships. Standardized scores placed her in the 99th percentile of academic and cognitive abilities. She had an abiding interest in physics and geometry, and would memorize passages from books with ease. ASD features were relatively mild, displayed mainly in poor eye contact, lack of attunement to social cues, failing to show empathy despite caring deeply about her peers and family, missing the humor in jokes, and seeming incapable of conversational banter. Conversation was notable for its pedantic tone, as if she was a little professor. Therapy focused on learning to read facial expressions, express empathy, maintain eye contact, and interpret social cues. Certain social principles were explicitly explained, while some social interactions were mirrored and practiced using engagement and challenge-based Theraplay activities. Sarah quickly applied her social play skills with her siblings, enjoying the lively social play. Conversational skills with peers were explained, role-played, and then practiced in vivo with other students. Developing a close friendship based on her new conversational skills was highly rewarding and self-reinforcing.

The cases of Tyler and Sarah highlight the diversity of the ASD world, the need for a range of therapeutic approaches, and how difficult it can be to choose the proper intervention approach for any individual child on the autism spectrum. Multiple functional skill domains may be affected, such as those spanning communication, domestic skills, self-care, community functioning, family functioning, personal recreation and leisure, health and wellness, community safety, and social reciprocity, to name just a few. Different therapeutic and teaching methods may be required for different domains. Furthermore, the autism spectrum interacts with the intellectual spectrum.

Therapy requires individualization for each child, and often the creativity to adapt known and proven methods to the specific situations encountered. Certain broad principles can be applied across all cases. Every child on the autism spectrum who presents as a student at a school or as a client at a clinic should be evaluated across the dimensions of communication, adaptive skills for everyday life, leisure repertoire, community integration, and social skills. However, in any area, needs and intervention may significantly diverge. To gain social and emotional capacities, for instance, the child may require a picture-based method of communication while practicing verbal and non-verbal communication skills for expressing empathy in a structured method. Some may benefit from receiving occupational therapy for sensory integration while experiencing non-verbal attunement, synchrony, and shared joy through Theraplay-based activities.

This book emphasizes the experience of the authors and other clinical service providers who have worked with children and youth on the autism spectrum, including those saddled with the combined struggle of ASD and cognitive limitations. Severe language limitations have also characterized many of the children and adolescents we have worked with over the years. Successes and setbacks when trying interventions have honed our awareness of what works for which children and families. Methods have included Theraplay, Applied Behavior Analysis (ABA) and behavior therapy, group therapy, social communication skills, specially designed educational and teaching curriculums, recreational therapy, and family therapy methods. Success has been found using a team approach, individualizing programs to the specific child, and charting what empirical findings or changes occur for each child. Integration of therapeutic methods has been the result of our experience and efforts, driven by what the children and families benefit from.

Sometimes a tense push–pull has existed between the use of relationship-rooted approaches such as Theraplay, which is firmly based on intrinsic social motivators, and the more practical, adaptive skills methods associated with behavior therapy, which has a tendency toward extrinsic reinforcement systems. This tension and the need for integration between the two models is highlighted and discussed in Chapter 2. Subsequent chapters provide the basic principles of both systems—Theraplay and Behavior Therapy—that are relevant to the effective support of children on the autism spectrum and their families. Key treatment needs across most children on the autism spectrum and with intellectual disability are discussed prior to chapters that delve into actual case studies,[1] with practical techniques, and descriptions of applied therapeutic methods. In addition, Chapter 6 on the Marschak Interaction Method (MIM) introduces the joint attention observational coding system for children on the autism spectrum, supplemental to the MIM. Chapter 12, the Theraplay activities chapter, introduces new activities and ways of tailoring Theraplay activities to meet clients' unique needs. Lastly, Chapter 13, by Dr. Susan Bundy-Myrow on using the traditional Theraplay approach for children on the autism spectrum, includes a composite case illustration.

The goal is for readers to gain meaningful knowledge and skills in practical methods they can utilize with the children in their own lives. The content is useful to therapists seeking to broaden their knowledge base, and it is clear enough that parents or caregivers[2] can immediately apply at least some of the methods described. However, it is impossible to fully describe all systems of therapy for ASD in one book—even a narrow band of interventions. Furthermore, skills cannot be fully obtained from a book. The work of coaching children, conducting therapy, teaching skills, and engaging in social interaction is an action-oriented, moment-to-moment experience. Ideas may be obtained from a book, but the actual dance of social interaction must be modeled and trained. To obtain the highest levels of success as a therapist, teacher, counselor, or parent or

---

1 Full consent has been obtained for cases described without alteration. Other cases have been anonymized and are composite cases.

2 In most cases, we have chosen to use the term "caregivers" to be an inclusive word, as children or youth may live with grandparents, foster families, aunts and uncles, or with guardians, and this book is written for all those who have the responsibility of raising a child on the autism spectrum.

caregiver, one may consider having an experienced supervisor and mentor to provide modeling and feedback.

Finally, please note that while The Theraplay Institute officially uses "practitioners" for Theraplay providers, in this book we use "therapists" and "clinicians" instead of "practitioners" to make the writing flow smoothly.

Chapter 2

The Need for Integrating Theraplay with Behavior Therapy

 Amanda, a developmental play therapist who uses Theraplay when working with children on the autism spectrum, is discussing treatment approaches with colleagues. She says:

> Avoid using behavior therapy with these children and their families. What these children need most is social engagement skills and what parents want most is a positive relationship with their children. Behavior therapy might be used to teach eye contact or shaking hands, but it just comes across as mechanical and awkward, and doesn't really help them gain a more intuitive sense of social exchanges. Furthermore, when parents use behavior therapy, they end up in power struggles with their child over multiple issues, the child ends up motivated only by edible rewards, and they all become frustrated by cumbersome charts. Expanding the parent and child's recreational activities that they do together socially has a much greater and more lasting impact on positive family functioning. And the child gains skills for playing with other children.

Amanda's colleagues nod in agreement and mentally swear never to get involved in behavior therapy programming.

Across town, Melanie, a behavior therapist, is training an in-home intervention team to do therapy with children on the autism spectrum. She tells her team:

The families we work with need concrete, evidence-based methods for teaching their children basic skills and communication strategies. If a child communicates more effectively, they will have fewer disruptive behaviors. Some parents want you to just play with their children, but that is not your job. Your job is to transfer skills to the parents by modeling methods of teaching independent living skills or demonstrating behavior management techniques. A critical goal is replacing disruptive behaviors with more adaptive ones.

The new team members nod their heads, confident that they are being taught the most scientific methods of treatment. They mentally swear to avoid getting caught up in frivolous play, and commit to being focused on teaching parents good positive reinforcement systems.

Members of both theoretical systems and camps who believe deeply in the effectiveness of their approaches express strong opinions. They seem to speak a completely different language. Theraplay therapists talk about attunement, emotional engagement, intersubjectivity, attachment cycles, and dimensions of the parent–child relationship. In contrast, behavior therapists speak in terms of primary and secondary reinforcers, functional assessment, conditioning, shaping, and operants of behavior. Is it possible that similar concepts are expressed beneath the linguistic differences between Theraplay and behavior therapists? Are the two groups addressing the same problems using different techniques, or are they focused on very different issues that demand different skill sets? Are the two models opposed so that one model can only be used to the exclusion of the other? Binary questions such as these are guaranteed to be misleading. However, answering such questions can lead to potent insights.

Therapists from both models work with children on the autism spectrum and support families. Both report dramatic successes, and both are painfully aware of spectacular failures. Both acknowledge that children need to build trusted relationships with adults. Both agree that children may lack emotional coping skills due to a lack of early parental care and modeling. The only primary difference is the method of handling a child's problems. Thus, this chapter intends to discuss key principles from Theraplay and behavior therapy to highlight the compatibility of the two models with the hope that all types of caregivers and professionals will expand their toolbox for assisting families and children on the autism spectrum.

Theraplay

Theraplay was developed around the principles of caregiver–child attachment and relationship needs. Due to its early cultivation as a method of working with children in Head Start,[1] Theraplay is also firmly grounded in practical early childhood education principles. Attachment research has demonstrated the importance of having a secure relationship with a responsive caregiver through infancy and childhood. Essential to a sense of security is the expectation that emotional, interactional, and physical needs will be met through the reliable, attuned, compassionate manner of a caregiver. Attunement refers to the ability of a caregiver to observe an infant or young child's non-verbal communication (eye contact, body tension, facial expressions, vocalizations, type of cry), to accurately interpret the intent of the communication, and then to respond to the child in a way that brings relief, satisfaction, or pleasure. If the cycle of communication–observation–interpretation–response–satisfaction is reliably completed with the caregiver over a period of months and years, the child learns to trust in relationships and develops skills in social reciprocity.

Early childhood education is centered round the developmental needs of young children as applied to learning new skills and functioning in a group setting. Physical, social, and learning needs and abilities are directed by physiological patterns of growth that determine cognitive functioning, motor skills, and emotional-social perspective. Learning occurs predominantly through exploration, movement, sensory experiences, and modeling of adults and peers. An emotionally safe environment is critical to learning and healthy social participation. Therapeutic applications

---

1   A program of the US Department of Health and Human Services that provides comprehensive early childhood education, health, nutrition, and parent involvement services to low-income children and families.

in Theraplay have drawn on these principles, training therapists to provide a clear structure to treatments, and arranging for mirroring and experiencing social engagement through various Theraplay activities based on early childhood repetitive, interactive, sensorimotor play.

Theraplay activities fall into four key relationship dimensions that guide Theraplay treatment—structure, engagement, nurture, and challenge:

- *Structure* refers to providing safety, organization, and regulation, both physically and emotionally. Physically, a room will be arranged to reduce distractions and promote safety. For instance, unnecessary toys are removed to focus on interactive play with the adult. A bean bag chair or comfortable cushions on the floor provide a sense of comfortable physical containment for the child while interacting with the therapist. Theraplay sequencing is utilized by the therapist for a clear plan of action, with goal-directed activities to meet the needs of the child. Emotional regulation is promoted by organizing a child's emotions with sensitive responses to the child's non-verbal cues. The therapist provides guidance and pacing of the session to create optimal arousal for the child.

- *Engagement* refers to creating shared joy, attuned interactions, and strong connections. The therapist focuses on creating "now moments" to connect with the child and to create the child's experience of seeing, hearing, and understanding. Non-verbal communication, such as facial expressions, voice tones, body gestures, etc., during fun, socially interactive activities naturally draws the child into the emotional engagement. In addition, social reciprocity is encouraged by the nature of the activities that require "serve and return."

- *Nurture* means promoting care, soothing, and attention to the child's attachment needs. Touch in various forms during nurture activities helps the child to feel sufficiently cared for. Nurture activities can be as simple as symbolically taking care of hurts by applying lotion, or regulating a highly aroused child with calm, firm pressure.

- *Challenge* references the need for children to learn and grow and feel empowered to attempt new things and to try new skills. The therapist assists the child in developing the ability to tolerate and carry out developmentally appropriate difficulties with various new activities by emphasizing cooperative and team play that could be crucial for social maturity.

Applied Behavior Analysis and Behavior Therapy

Applied Behavior Analysis (ABA) is the evaluation process for assessing the reasons that a person engages in any behavior. While behavior therapy refers to the principles and procedures for promoting behavioral change— for example, if a child was highly avoidant of brushing their teeth, but unable to verbally explain why—ABA might be used to study the situation and understand the barriers to teeth brushing. In one such situation, the clinicians had the child taste-test different dental pastes, discovering that the child had extreme dislike for the taste of mint. By changing the toothpaste flavor (e.g., to cinnamon or bubble gum), the child became willing to regularly brush their teeth. The process of ABA involves careful observation, interview of people who know the person well, and short, experimental trials to determine the nature of the problem. When done correctly and respectfully, this process improves understanding of the individual in need and the situational factors that contribute to the difficulty, and it can improve caregiver and service-provider empathy for the person's struggle and suffering. It can set the stage for effective intervention to change the situation.

Behavior therapy refers to the various interventions that may be utilized to assist with learning new skills, with new habit creation, and with avoiding negative or harmful behaviors. It was developed on the premise of learning and conditioning. All organisms, including humans, organize their behavior around meeting various needs that range from basic safety to satisfying curiosity. Basic needs include food, warmth, touch, water, and freedom from pain. Higher level needs include social interaction, communicating thoughts or feelings, and engaging in play or activities for fun. Key behavioral principles important to therapeutic intervention include the following:

- *Reinforcement:* When a person is motivated to engage in some action to gain an object (e.g., food) or experience (e.g., skiing), that object or experience is said to be positively reinforcing. If a person engages in the behavior to stop pain (e.g., getting a hug for comfort), the stopping of discomfort is said to be negatively reinforcing. Some experiences are aversive, and may cause a person to stop a behavior; for example, getting poison ivy rash can be pretty punishing and could cause a person to refrain from walking through certain wooded regions. Some learning occurs through direct experience, while other learning occurs through watching others, called vicarious learning, or learning through modeling. Most learning occurs over multiple trials and slow approximations of success.

- *Shaping:* Shaping is the process of guiding learning in small steps toward greater competence. Successive approximation of a target behavior toward an ultimate goal will lead to the change. Habit creation is the development of behavior patterns that become highly routine and automatic through constant use. Skillfully applied behavior therapy uses various combinations of these principles to help children and adults increase their social skills, independent living skills, and healthy habits. Conversely, harmful behavior patterns can be diminished through such therapy strategies as promoting and reinforcing alternative actions and healthier choices.

- *Conditioning:* Humans are susceptible to sensory information in their environment and social cues. We are motivated to avoid harm or pain and seek safety or comfort. Behavioral science has demonstrated how certain behaviors can be strongly conditioned. For instance, during World War II, hearing an airplane overhead was associated with frightening bombs dropping in many European cities. People learned to drop down and seek cover. Years later, a family friend who had been a child living in Europe during the war was surprised by a military jet flyover before a parade here, in America. He automatically dropped to the ground and crawled under a picnic table. This automatic, conditioned response has great survival value, but it is also the basis for reactions to post-traumatic stress disorder (PTSD). A similar direct or vicarious conditioning process can be partly responsible for developing phobias and other anxiety disorders. Behavior therapy can effectively offer counter-conditioning and anxiety reduction by teaching coping skills, and supportively guiding people through exposure and effectively handling the feared situations.

Many experiences are only pleasurable by the nature of learning and conditioning. For example, many people find earning money reinforcing, meaning they change their behavior and put forth great effort to obtain it. However, money has no inherent value, being made of inedible and nearly worthless materials. People develop a strong affinity for this commodity through common societal agreement and years of social training. People learn that it can be exchanged for things with intrinsic value, like food. These types of motivators are called secondary reinforcers. Some secondary reinforcers are non-tangible things, like social status. Most behavior has a complex array of motivators. For example, a skiing vacation may be motivated by intrinsic interest in the experiences of fast movement down a mountain and by a secondary reinforcer of bragging rights for visiting an exotic location.

Integration of Theraplay and Behavior Therapy

Some similarities between Theraplay and behavior therapy may be immediately apparent. Both emphasize the importance of therapists' modeling skills ("mirroring" in Theraplay) for the clients or the caregivers they train. Both emphasize feedback to the learner (caregiver or child) to shape ("change" in Theraplay) the individual toward success in using the skills ("experience" in Theraplay) practiced. This similarity begs the question—why would two therapies with different terminology emphasize the same learning process of modeling and response? Logically, this is because this method works so well and is the basis for human learning. From the earliest stages of life, humans learn by observing, imitating, and receiving feedback. For example, an infant will imitate a caregiver's facial expressions, gestures, and body movements, and the response is the attention, stimulation, and social interaction the caregiver provides in return. This process is at the core of social learning, as demonstrated in experiments by Ed Tronick (2011). As infants and toddlers grow, they observe the behavior modeled by caregivers and siblings, learning some behaviors vicariously. Practice is then required to fine-tune their motor skills; feedback is the result obtained. Only as older children and adults do we try to learn by reading or merely hearing an explanation. The most effective learning from childhood through old age is learning by observing a model, practicing the action, and then receiving corrective responses from the environment or another person.

Specific experiences are intrinsically pleasurable or painful by their very nature. No training is required for an infant to realize that being hugged and held feels good, and that milk tastes good and takes away hunger. No training is needed for an infant to recognize that being stabbed by a needle is painful. Experiences rooted in solid biological drives that motivate people to action are said to be intrinsic or primary reinforcers, including food, warmth, touch, social interaction, exploration, and movement, among others. Attachment-based needs fall into this category and have complex social behaviors that promote a caregiver–child emotional connection. This is intrinsically reinforced by a caregiver cuddling with, holding, looking at, and seeing the smiles of the infant. The same things reinforce the infant's social behavior—the infant or toddler uses the caregivers as a secure safety base. Powerful hormones, touch receptors, neurotransmitters, and pleasure-seeking brain systems govern this process for both the child and caregiver.

Although understanding terminology differences on how to reinforce behavior and the most important motivators may generate understanding between Theraplay therapists and behavior therapists, apparent differences exist. First, despite the indispensable nature of intrinsic and extrinsic reinforcers in human behavior, the distinctive emphasis on applying intrinsic and extrinsic reinforcers needs to be noted. Theraplay emphasizes intrinsic reinforcement that often implies motivators internal to the animal or person, something done purely "for fun or personal interest." Animal ethnologist Konrad Lorenz (1961) explained the meaning of intrinsic motivation using a jackdaw that flew up and down in a natural wind tunnel on his farm. Unable to find any practical reason for the behavior, he concluded that the bird did it for pure enjoyment—for fun; in other words, it was intrinsically reinforcing. Likewise, listening to stories, reading novels, and engaging in social conversation or board games are activities many humans do out of intrinsic motivation, mainly for fun. Theraplay therapists believe that new, focused, attuned interactions through Theraplay provide opportunities for the child to create intrinsic motivation for positive changes. Yet intrinsic motivation has some limitations when supporting children on the autism spectrum toward behavioral change. This is due to their difficulty integrating the cycle of sensory input–cognitive and emotional process–motor execution (action). For instance, after playing cotton ball hide-and-seek (sensory input) in Theraplay, a neurotypical child with attachment issues starts translating shared joy and attuned reciprocity with a caregiver as a rewarding experience (thought–feeling process). The realization of this new positive experience can intrinsically motivate the child to seek positive interactions by reducing cranky behavior (motor execution). Yet children on the autism spectrum, struggling with social cues, often need an additional and concrete extrinsic motivator to execute learning into action, which we believe behavior therapy can contribute.

Behavior therapy strongly supports extrinsic reinforcement, which refers to motivators external to a person or done for secondary gain. For example, taking a class you are not interested in but need for graduation from school is an example of extrinsic motivation. Doing chores to receive an allowance is another example of an extrinsic motivator. For some children, playing a cotton ball hide-and-seek game to reward stopping cranky behavior might be effective. In this case, playing a cotton ball hide-and-seek game becomes an extrinsic motivator, although Theraplay therapists may abhor using Theraplay activities as an extrinsic motivator.

Rakeem's case provides a short illustration of integrating Theraplay and behavior therapy.

Rakeem had both very severe autistic features and very severe intellectual delays. As a result, learning new skills took high repetition over a much longer time. Educationally, he progressed slowly and hit clear limits in his ability to understand numbers or recognize letters. Reading was limited to recognizing safety signs around the community (e.g., "Stop," "Bathroom," "Walk," "Danger"), even into adolescence. Theraplay helped Rakeem greatly expand his recreational repertoire and ability to socially engage with other people. Although he could play with others or go on community outings with prompting and supervision, his interest in socializing with any particular person remained limited. On the other hand, through much practice with behavior therapy, he developed adequate skills to live in a group home, take care of his own self-care needs, and have meaningful supported employment activities in the community.

Chapter 3

Theraplay and Its Relevance to Children on the Autism Spectrum

 At age 20, Geoffrey was still living in a residential treatment program that provided specialized communication training for his limited verbal skills, specialized education to promote self-care and vocational skills, and supervised community integration trips. In periods of frustration, Geoffrey could become very aggressive, making it very hard for him to live safely at home. A clear schedule, structured routine, and attentive staff to provide coaching and communication support were essential to his learning and to calm his participation in group activities. Behavior therapy techniques helped him develop communication skills, engage in schoolwork completion, participate in self-care, and use a few rote social behaviors, such as greetings. However, Geoffrey had only one preferred recreational activity—playing catch with any kind of ball. Outside of this, his social interaction was limited. Thus, Theraplay was added to promote social and relationship skills that could help improve family interaction.

Geoffrey's enjoyment of catching and throwing was leveraged to expand his repertoire of social activities as two therapists developed a social relationship with him. In an early individual session, one therapist tossed Geoffrey a ribbon ball (something new to him), causing Geoffrey to laugh, reciprocate with throwing, and reach out for a high five. The second therapist walked in (a surprise) with an enthusiastic "Hello, Geoffrey!" giving him another high five, and then saying, "What did you bring with you? Let me take a look at your hands." Smiling, Geoffrey allowed the therapist to count his fingers. Appearing bashful, Geoffrey kept his head down and eyes averted; using a cheerful, enthusiastic voice, the therapist counted more fingers, "One, two, three, four, five!" and leaned down close to Geoffrey's face to peer into his eyes. Geoffrey responded by looking up and spontaneously raising his hand for another high five, and then looking up and around as the therapist counted his other fingers and then noticed his ears. Next, Geoffrey spontaneously opened his mouth to show his teeth, eliciting the therapist's comment, "Oh, you brought your teeth." The therapist transitioned into blowing bubbles for Geoffrey, with the first therapist demonstrating how to pop bubbles. Imitating the therapist, Geoffrey also popped bubbles, clapped a bubble with the therapist, listened to a bubble pop on his ear, and learned to blow his own bubbles for the first time.

Geoffrey practiced turn-taking and waiting for a countdown while he and the two therapists played a game of dropping a beanie animal from the top of each person's head into another person's hand. Next, the therapists switched to helping Geoffrey make hand prints on paper with lotion and powder, to which he smiled, although he kept his eyes averted. Increased interest and eye contact were finally established when Geoffrey placed his hands on either side of a balloon to feel it expand with the therapist's blowing. Peering over the balloon, he made a few moments of warm eye contact, followed by a lively exchange of hitting the balloon back and forth with one of the therapists. Taking turns with balloon hitting was transitioned into sharing moments of joy by meeting Geoffrey's sensory needs with a hand print pin board, blowing feathers to each other, and cooperatively squishing therapy putty. Geoffrey spontaneously offered the sensory board to the other therapist in the spirit of turn-taking, showing he had grasped the social sequence.

This case demonstrates the use of Theraplay as a tool for emotional engagement, social skill teaching, and expanding a young person's repertoire of social leisure activities. In the early years of autism research and treatment, Austin DesLauriers and Carole Carlson (1969) recognized that the critical and most disabling aspect of autism was the deficiency in social awareness and lack of social engagement skills. Ivar Lovaas and James Simmons (1969) were already doing promising work in shaping specific behaviors and skills through behavioral principles. DesLauriers and Carlson noted that strict behavioral shaping could result in performing an action without social intent or flexibility. Believing that autism was a neurological impairment, they considered the available evidence for how humans develop flexible social skills in the first place. Donald Winnicott's work (1965) on parenting influenced their thinking, as did John Bowlby's work on attachment (1969). Both Winnicott and Bowlby emphasized parent–child interaction as critical to healthy social-emotional development, prompting DesLauriers and Carlson to design a play-based program that promoted intensive developmental social play between adult staff and children on the severe end of the autism spectrum in a residential center.

Children in the center were intellectually delayed and with limited verbal or abstract reasoning skills, in addition to being on the autism spectrum. None in their group had imaginary play skills, demonstrating the repetitive and stereotyped play typical for children on the autism spectrum. Thus, DesLauriers and Carlson believed that social interactions should model infants' or toddlers' early developmental play interactions with mothers. The play was designed to include high sensory input, including touch, close face-to-face interaction with exaggerated facial expression, and a lilting voice showing interest and amazement. Few toys were used, as the caregiver was emphasized as being the most exciting source of stimulation. Its impact on the children was remarkable. Documenting change over the course of a year, the children demonstrated gains in social interaction, behavioral regulation, and participation in adaptive self-care skills.

Having shared their methods with a small number of other therapists and psychologists, Theraplay might have remained a footnote in the treatment of autism had it not been for the work of Ann Jernberg and Phyllis Booth (2001). Adapting the DesLauriers and Carlson methods, they successfully used them as an early model for providing mental health treatment to emotionally impaired children on the Head Start program

(Jernberg, Hurst, & Lyman 1969, 1975). The emphasis on early childhood developmental play and healthy caregiving proved exceptionally successful. Initially used for individual therapy, therapists soon realized that the model of training caregiving staff in the school to assist a difficult child as a secure base of emotional strength could be provided in a family therapy context. As a result, the parent became part of the therapeutic system, receiving guidance and mentoring from clinicians to improve their interaction skills with their child (Jernberg 1984).

After working with John Bowlby for a year, Phyllis Booth brought an enhanced emphasis on caregiver–child attachment to Theraplay work. Strengthening attachment between a caregiver and child became an essential component of the Theraplay model, and its efficacy for enhancing attachment was well documented in case studies and clinical reports. In addition to being recognized as a useful method for working with children in foster care (Mäkelä & Vierikko 2004), post-adoption (Bostrom 1995), or situations where disruptive, defiant behavior was related to parenting difficulty (Booth & Koller 1998), there was also evidence that Theraplay helped children with internalizing disorders (Siu 2009; Wettig, Coleman, & Geider 2011). Success in these arenas led to international recognition and eclipsed the earlier beginnings of Theraplay as an intervention for children on the autism spectrum.

Relatively recent work has returned to studying Theraplay as a method for helping children on the autism spectrum or with developmental disabilities (Azoulay 2000; Siu 2014). A case study using Theraplay for developmentally delayed children showed that Theraplay was associated with increased attention, responsiveness, and relatedness to others (Azoulay 2000). Angela Siu (2014) demonstrated that Theraplay group intervention for children with developmental disabilities significantly improved their social skills, particularly social communication, while Susan Bundy-Myrow (2000) described the use of Group Theraplay specifically for children on the autism spectrum. Joseph Franklin *et al.* (2007) demonstrated promising outcomes in using Theraplay with families and their children on the autism spectrum, and Amanda Hiles Howard *et al.* (2018) found that a two-week intensive program for parents and their children on the autism spectrum could improve parent–child social interaction across multiple dimensions of interaction, such as affective engagement, joint attention, and social cooperation.

Theraplay principles for children on the autism spectrum

The benefit to children on the autism spectrum from the Theraplay model comes in fostering social skills and strengthening relationships. While behavioral interventions such as Applied Behavior Analysis (ABA) or Discrete Trial Training (DTT) are recognized as evidence-based models for children on the autism spectrum, relationship and play-based interventions, such as DIRFloortime® and play therapy, are interventions with emerging evidence (Lindgren & Doobay 2011). Play-oriented skills are an essential way to develop children's learning of social communication and practicing social rules. Theraplay principles guide the therapist in making Theraplay optimally effective for both caregiver and child.

Theraplay involves both therapeutic and parenting techniques. The therapist provides sessions lasting from 30 to 90 minutes in which an array of activities are utilized for interacting with a child or training a caregiver, during which specific skills are worked on. Parenting techniques are developed through a highly collaborative process with caregivers. A focus is placed on guiding caregivers to interact with the child daily, following Theraplay principles. Eight helpful Theraplay principles for children on the autism spectrum are as follows: (1) create an environment of social and emotional safety; (2) promote social engagement through face-to-face contact; (3) enhance social reciprocity with joint attention; (4) emphasize non-verbal interaction; (5) experience play and socialization at the child's development level; (6) utilize multisensory stimulation; (7) promote emotional regulation and self-control; and (8) activate mirror neurons in a naturalistic way.

1. Create an environment of social and emotional safety

The recent discovery of the "smart vagus" in the brain (Porges 2011) offers a scientific understanding of why we need to build a social and emotional safety net in therapy. By traveling through specific parts of our bodies, such as the face, heart, and visceral areas, the "smart vagus" connects the face and the heart and helps us know if we are in a safe condition to connect with others. Theraplay generates an environment of social and emotional safety in which social skills and new play skills can be developed and practiced. In traditional academic or counseling situations, children often experience therapists or teachers pressuring them to talk about problems or complete increasingly difficult educational tasks. Talk avoidance is a common reaction to task frustration. Theraplay-based therapy starts with activities that are simple yet enjoyable, focusing on experiencing social interaction as safe and enjoyable. The socially and emotionally safe physiological conditions are theorized to eventually permit extensive networks of nerves in the heart and the digestive system to send and/or receive complex information through the interplay between brain and body (Badenoch 2011; Baldini *et al.* 2014), and to promote emotional regulation.

2. Promote social engagement through face-to-face contact

Theraplay explicitly addresses the needs of children on the autism spectrum within the social development model. It is inherently social and helps a child become emotionally engaged with another human through face-to-face contact. While adults tend to emphasize linguistic verbal exchanges (talking) as the dominant social currency, social skills are first learned prior to acquiring language. A caregiver and baby will dynamically interact through facial expression, reaching, pointing, cooing, using lilting, non-word vocal tones, touching, and shared eye contact (Tronick 2011). An infant demonstrates sensitivity to vocal rhythm, pauses, and emotional expression well before language develops. Within three months, an infant already demonstrates intuitive knowledge of social dynamics. Theraplay is designed to model and highlight these diverse skills in the service of helping children on the autism spectrum.

Children on the autism spectrum typically have difficulties expressing themselves and have impaired social interaction development, manifesting as inaccurate prosody, rhythm, and intonation. Children with autism who have limited cognitive skills often have limited verbal skills, as well. Both receptive and expressive language may be impaired, and reading of facial expressions is often poor. Children with autism who have high cognitive skills may nevertheless struggle to read facial expressions or interpret tone of voice. Theraplay, which facilitates social engagement through face-to-face contact, offers an opportunity for children on the autism spectrum to improve their ability to understand non-verbal cues from others. By emphasizing non-verbal social interaction and play that is at a less abstract level, a caregiver and child can have more rewarding social exchanges and more mutually satisfying recreational moments together. In our case illustration, Geoffrey and the two therapists enjoyed over 12 different social games (from catch to cooperative bubble popping to hand prints to feather blowing), representing an expansion of Geoffrey's social interaction repertoire from his single standard game (ball toss) to multiple activities involving turn-taking and shared experience. These activities were subsequently used to include Geoffrey in peer group interactions and parent–child interactions.

3. Enhance social reciprocity with joint attention

Theraplay promotes social reciprocity. Children on the autism spectrum often fail to recognize the desires and needs of the people around them, missing out on key opportunities to help others, give back, and connect through moments of sharing with another. Children with autism tend to show high rigidity in thinking, and play with restricted interests and limited social interaction. The bidirectional nature of Theraplay activities increases these children's opportunities to reciprocate social bids, creating rewarding social pleasure in the exchange. Children with more significant functional limitations may be assisted with self-care activities and have many treatments done to them unidirectionally, following the medical model. For instance, an occupational therapist may provide deep-pressure sensory input, but rarely would the child be asked to reciprocate. Within the confines of the Theraplay model, sensory activities with Geoffrey were shared with his therapists. Together they felt a sensory pin board, each putting a hand on either side and shifting it back and forth. Bubbles were blown for Geoffrey, and he was then guided to blow some back.

During a reciprocal interaction, joint attention is promoted. Joint attention is the coordinated and shared focus two or more people simultaneously have on an object or subject. This concept is the basis for pointing at things, commenting on the world, shared laughter, and working together on a task in a coordinated manner. The therapist works to connect with the child's world, creating moments of joint attention and shared experience, starting with focusing on the young person's physical being. For example, one of the therapists brought Geoffrey to joint attention by dramatically noting Geoffrey's fingers and ears. Geoffrey responded by showing his teeth—perhaps because the therapist had leaned in close to look at his face.

Joint attention is the basis for responding appropriately in social situations and following a social sequence. Geoffrey eventually showed that he followed a social sequence. He and one of the therapists shared an experiential moment of feeling a sensory pin board, after which Geoffrey passed the pin board to the other therapist who had yet to feel it. Instead of a sensory treatment being "done to" Geoffrey, it was "done with" Geoffrey in the context of shared social experience. With practice, children on the autism spectrum become aware of these basic social contingencies and generalize the value of joint attention to other situations, such as getting someone's attention to point to the desired food instead of just taking it or becoming aggressive.

4. Emphasize non-verbal interaction

Social reciprocity in Theraplay often happens non-verbally. Non-verbal interaction is emphasized, making it accessible to all people. Talk therapy is heavily emphasized across the mental health world due to its history as a method of supporting people in sharing feelings, problem solving, challenging maladaptive thoughts, and planning for behavioral changes. For all these reasons, it is of severely limited use (and often no use) for individuals on the severe end of the autism scale, language deficiency, and moderate to severe intellectual delay. Lack of abstract thinking and linguistic sophistication limit the usage of talk therapies for children on the autism spectrum. Defiance and non-compliance caused by rigidity can interfere with talk therapy applications, even when the child has advanced intellectual skills. In contrast, Theraplay's fun, challenging, and emotionally engaging play sequences often entice higher-functioning children with defiant behavior into the therapy process, opening up avenues for building trust with the therapist. The developmental activities and emphasis on non-verbal interaction make this therapy highly accessible for neurodiverse children, those with less cognitive capacity, and those with limited verbal and social skills.

Emphasis on non-verbal interaction also creates opportunities to help children on the autism spectrum experience and learn emotions that are exaggerated and highlighted during Theraplay. Children with autism who can explain their experience will often report that they struggle to see or interpret the emotions on other people's faces. Research has demonstrated the tendency of children with autism to have trouble integrating emotional information from the entire face, even despite otherwise strong cognitive skills (Wang *et al.* 2007). Some social skills training programs will practice naming emotions in pictures or videos. While a Theraplay therapist may also use this, a strong emphasis is placed on being very expressive in real time. Helping the child to have repeated experiences with clearly seeing emotional reactions is a component of treatment. By using an exaggerated facial expression or vocal sound, Theraplay therapists work to capture the attention of children on the autism spectrum. Two-person (dyadic) fun Theraplay activities are at the heart of enticing these children to attend to social cues. For instance, a therapist may use an exaggerated facial expression as a signal to drop a bean bag off of their head into the child's hand or to punch through a sheet of newspaper.

In Geoffrey's case, the two therapists used highly expressive and exaggerated facial expressions along with high modulation of vocal tone to demonstrate their reactions to his interactions. They often moved their faces close to his, attracting his attention. Specific activities were designed to elicit natural eye gaze, such as having Geoffrey put his hands on a balloon a therapist was blowing up, causing them to make eye contact over the balloon.

It should be noted that eye contact should never be forced or demanded. Many people on the autistic spectrum find eye contact uncomfortable or distressing. However, in the context of enjoyable and safe social engagement, enjoyment of eye contact can increase and feel more comfortable. Pairing a warm and engaging social interaction with eye contact can represent a way to desensitize eye contact and build tolerance for this social behavior. While eye contact may never feel completely comfortable for some individuals, practice in a naturalistic manner can help them utilize this method of social engagement and communication more effectively in daily life.

5. Experience play and socialization at the child's development level

Theraplay meets the child at a specific developmental level of play and socialization. As Daniel Siegel stated, "attachment relationships are important in the unfolding of the emotional and social development of the child during the early years of life" (2001, p.71). Receiving attachment-based Theraplay activities at the child's specific developmental level of play and socialization promotes the positive development of social skills. Geoffrey's intellectual and social development was, in many respects, below that of a five-year-old. It was unlikely that he would ever see the purpose behind a board game, much less comprehend the rules. The disconnect between advancing age and limited cognitive and social development often results in parents or other caregivers lacking activities for mutual enjoyment. By introducing social leisure activities within his developmental capacity, Geoffrey was able to experience success and some fun, evidenced in his laughing and smiling, high fives, and occasional eye contact.

Additionally, the games played with Geoffrey were generally enjoyable for all ages. Some activities, such as tossing a beanie animal back and forth, were leveraged into beanie throwing games, similar to bean bag throwing games played by adults at backyard parties and football games. Theraplay gave Geoffrey a socially interactive and even age-appropriate activity to do with people of all ages.

Theraplay is a highly useful method for getting to know a child as a person through mutually fun interaction. Beyond its value for teaching social skills, the core value of Theraplay is its facilitation of a relationship between the child and adult (caregiver, teacher, therapist). When we started using Theraplay activities with the children in our care who were on the spectrum, we noted an immediate shift in the relationship dynamic, a shift toward connection and enjoyment of shared time between both child and therapist. The experience was no longer about teaching, but about sharing meaningful time together. One father stated that Theraplay helped him and the rest of the family experience a relationship with his son/their brother on the autism spectrum that was based on mutual caring and intrinsic social enjoyment rather than on some type of behavior change. The brother (on the autism spectrum) and younger sister specifically built a relationship in which they both enjoyed playing games and singing songs together, something that was meaningful to both of them.

6. Utilize multisensory stimulation

Occupational therapists who attend Theraplay training find that almost all Theraplay activities can be easily used to help children work on the sensory integration process. An emphasis on multisensory stimulation in Theraplay meets the sensory needs of many children on the autism spectrum who need supportive touch, vestibular input, or other sensory experiences. Distinctively tactile materials such as lotion, baby powder, cotton balls, balloons, blankets, bubbles, newspapers, feathers, pillows, foils, scarfs, or shaving creams are typically used. Theraplay therapists will deliver activities with voice sound effects, songs, and action words, like "slippery, slippery, slip" to applying lotion, "clap, clap, clap" to patty cake, "swoosh, swoosh" to rolling up sleeves, or even making the sneeze sound of "achoo" to hit a balloon together. Theraplay involves all the senses that integrate social connection with tactile experience with brief verbal expression. Rocking, blanket swing, patting on the back, talking in soothing tones, holding firmly, fanning, singing, giving a piggyback ride, or feeding represent archetypes of the Theraplay avenue of sensory input. Theraplay activities combine vestibular input, touch (vibration, warmth, deep pressure), sound, and even smell.

Of course, the multisensory aspect of Theraplay activities must be used with sensitivity to avoid adverse reactions. Some children on the autism spectrum may not be neurologically equipped to encode particular sensory input positively. Since autism is particularly associated with sensory hyperactivity or sensitivity, finding ways to accommodate sensory needs is a valuable part of the practice. Accommodation to sensory input with a positive relational experience in Theraplay is key to keeping these children from their natural tendency of isolation. Theraplay therapists investigate which sensory experiences are most helpful to a specific child, and they then train caregivers to provide this type of input safely and at the right time. For example, some children we have worked with have experienced improved sleep by having a weighted or heavy blanket at night, and one girl we have worked with demands that her mother gives her a deep-pressure massage every day to calm her stress level.

Geoffrey was engaged in all these types of integrative sensory plays with the therapists during the months of his therapy. This included artwork with lotion or finger paint, balancing while holding a therapist's hand, cooperative play with novel tactile objects (squishy balls, feathers, therapy putty, a pin board), tactile experiences such as writing on his back or hand, smelling lotions, drinks, or fruit snacks before eating, and swinging with the therapists, to name a few. These activities engaged his interest, making him more willing to engage with the therapists socially.

7. Promote emotional regulation and self-control

Siegel (2001, p.81) wrote, "from the beginning of life, 'self-regulation' is determined in part by an interactive 'dyadic' process of mutual co-regulation." Emotional regulation is first learned in the context of caregiver–child relationships. An infant is assisted in regulating input by an attuned caregiver who notices stress and responds to change the environment or increase physical support to the child. Throughout life, regulation generally occurs most successfully in the context of social support rather than isolation.

Along with fostering attachment, Theraplay inherently promotes emotional regulation, self-regulation, and impulse control. Having boisterous and quiet activities alternating in the sequence of a Theraplay session provides opportunities for children and their caregivers to work on adjusting arousal levels. The structure and nurture dimensions of Theraplay help children on the autism spectrum practice impulse control. For instance, squeezing each finger as a nurture activity may calm the child with high arousal. During a structure activity of hand stack, a child may be guided to put their hands on top only when their name is called. By alternating hands to make a stack, a therapist deliberately calls out the child's name slowly or fast, to help them work on gaining impulse control. A mummy wrap activity is another example. This activity is not only fun, but it could give a mission to the child to be still by saying, for example, "Sam, a mummy has a special power not to move until it hears 'cheeseburger,' which is its favorite food. I wonder if you could become a mummy by being still like a statue while I wrap you around with this toilet paper?" Children on the autism spectrum often fail to accomplish this mission at first. In which case, the activity is broken down, like wrapping around arms or legs in the beginning, and gradually wrapping around the child's whole body once they gain better control over their body.

Geoffrey tended to throw balls much too hard, so we worked on self-control in throwing at different speeds. We also worked on the skill of waiting to do an activity until a signal (a word or hand signal) was given. After that, Geoffrey effectively learned to pause and take redirection.

8. Activate mirror neurons in a naturalistic way

Mirror neurons are naturally activated through Theraplay games. The human brain has circuits that read another person's actions, mapping the actions onto the observer's brain, which enables us to imitate other people, a critical aspect of learning life skills. Socially, it helps humans mirror another person's emotional expression, responding with empathy. The mirror neuron system is critical because it guides social behavior. It also allows a person to engage in perspective taking, modeling others, and to experience empathy, all of which are important to social-emotional relationships with others (Iacoboni 2007, 2009). According to Lindsay Oberman and colleagues at the University of California, San Diego (2005), individuals on the autism spectrum tend to have abnormal functional mirror neuron systems. In other words, children on the autism spectrum may present difficulties interpreting other people's physical or emotional intent, as being able to model another person's actions internally or facial expression gives us clues to its meaning.

Many Theraplay games center on imitation and coordinated action with another person. Indeed, the mirror game does this directly. A therapist facing the child moves their arms and body in different ways while the child pretends to be a mirror, copying the movements exactly. Some Theraplay therapists in Korea even utilize a large wall mirror to stimulate mirror neuron functioning during Theraplay activities. Other games require cooperative work, such as having child–adult legs tied together for a three-legged walk. In our clinical experience, children start very awkward with such activities, but quickly increase their ability to coordinate efforts with another person. In some cases, this ability is further transferred into working with another person in a more integrated manner to get chores done or participate in a team game.

Geoffrey was engaged in various imitation games with the therapists. This involved cooperative games of hand clapping, three-legged walking, and pulling each other up from a seated position. It also involved copying the therapists in activities, such as high-fiving a bubble together, balancing something on both parties' heads, or mirror-type games. He was able to learn through these skills, thereby increasing his social repertoire.

Conclusion

Theraplay can be used across social dimensions, promoting practical recreational skills, social reciprocity, and emotional connection with a play partner. As illustrated in Geoffrey's case, Theraplay promotes social-emotional health from a neurobiological standpoint, emphasizing the use of mirroring and imitation. It also promotes behavioral change through enhanced self-control and emotional regulation. In Geoffrey's case, he progressed to using his increased range of social engagement activities with various residential staff. Geoffrey's mother participated in many activities with him under the therapist's guidance. He eventually graduated from the program and moved into a supported-living group home with roommates.

Chapter 4

Critical Therapeutic Domains for Youth on the Autism Spectrum in Residential Care

 Zoey ran back and forth across his home lounge area in the residential treatment center. He would walk a few steps, dart the rest of the way, and then stop and consider the piece of string in his hand, flapping it rapidly back and forth. Flapping would continue for 30 or 40 seconds while standing in place, and then he would walk with lunging strides across the room, seemingly oblivious to his two peers sitting on a sofa watching TV. The unit psychologist and I (A. Rand Coleman) called Zoey's name, getting a glance in response, but he mostly seemed to ignore us as he watched the string flip in his hand. Then, finally, he smiled, seemingly at nothing.

"Hi Zoey," I said, walking up to him. "Can I see your string?"

He allowed me to look at the string briefly, but took it back and darted away. However, a blown-up balloon shortly got his attention. Zoey tapped it without directing any attention to me, and then walked away to his room to lie down.

"I think our session is over," I said to the other psychologist. It had lasted about five minutes and seemed to have generated no social interaction between Zoey and ourselves. Indeed, it was unclear whether he had noticed us, except that he had removed his string from my grasp.

Zoey highlighted the struggles and social behavior of youth on the severe end of the autism spectrum with whom we worked in our intensive residential treatment program. His play was limited to repetitive and stereotyped actions ("stereotyped" referring to sequences of movement done repetitively without apparent meaning or functional utility). Zoey particularly liked to flick and flap string or paper. Imaginary play was absent and social interaction was rare. He might notice an item some other person was holding. Still, his noticing lacked the sense of collaboration or mutual attention usually present when one person shares an item, food, picture, or thought with another. In other words, he showed minimal joint attention (the sharing of interest in something with another person).

Zoey had profound limited communication skills. At age 18, most verbalization was limited to grunts, with a hand gesture to indicate what he wanted. He had learned the basic use of a picture communication system in which he would give a picture card to an adult to indicate an item he desired. He had better receptive skills, demonstrated by his following of staff or parent directives to participate in washing and grooming, dressing, basic chores, and safety commands. Despite years of intensive speech therapy efforts, expressive language skills had never developed, except for using pictures. His interests were minimal. While Zoey did puzzles when encouraged to do so by the therapeutic staff, there was no sense that he derived the pleasure from this that a person might derive from a simple hobby.

Defining the treatment parameters

Zoey's situation highlights the multiple need domains of treatment for youth on the severe end of the autism spectrum. Case conceptualization and treatment planning are typically straightforward in traditional outpatient therapy with more typically developing adults or children. A relatively intact social awareness and a typically developing cognitive level may be counted on. The problem will normally be defined in terms of one or two psychiatric disorders (e.g., depression, anxiety, post-traumatic stress disorder (PTSD), obsessive-compulsive disorder (OCD)) or a specific life need (e.g., improving a marital relationship, handling stress at work, coping with pain, improving parenting skills). A therapeutic model is often decided on along with a number of intervention techniques. In contrast, youth such as Zoey may have difficulties across many life domains, so no one approach or therapeutic model will be adequate.

Due to many concerns for our youth in residential care, it was necessary to define what it meant to 'do' good therapy. Some team members emphasized communication, while others emphasized reducing disruptive behavior. Yet others wanted to focus primarily on teaching adaptive skills for independent living. Treatment focus tended to depend on the team member's training and roles with the youth. Team members from all parts of the support system (e.g., treatment manager, teacher, social services coordinator, psychologist, program coordinator) conducted intensive reviews of the youth's needs at the center. As a result, various concerns were clustered in more operationally defined, functional parameters to target effective therapy and educational efforts. The identified parameters are helpful to guide directions for staff training programs, development or acquisition of therapeutic materials, and design of educational and residential support plans.

The typical five critical domains for therapeutic support are: (1) social interaction and relationship skills; (2) social communication skills; (4) adaptive skills for everyday living; (4) social and personal leisure and recreational skills; and (5) community integration.

1. Social interaction and relationship skills

Poor social skills most strongly characterize autism, arguably the most disabling issue. The human world is inherently social, as the ability to coordinate our efforts with others is critical to our survival as mammals that must learn almost every skill. Social interaction requires skills from simple to complex, including giving eye contact at the right times and to the right degree, noticing what other people notice and responding to this, interpreting facial expressions, responding to subtle changes in facial expression, body posture, or gesture, appreciating the emotional impact an event has on another person, and expressing empathy, care, or affection. Healthy relationships require reciprocity between partners. Avoiding harm and making social decisions involves a theory of mind—

knowing that others could have a different perspective from your own, different needs, and different emotional responses.

2. Social communication skills

Communication through language and gesture is a hallmark of human interaction. At the earliest age, after verbal names for things are learned, infants and toddlers use explicit naming and gestures to indicate what they want, predicated partly on joint attention and theory of mind. The infant becomes aware that caregiver attention can be drawn to the same item the infant wants, first through gesture or eye gaze, and then through words. The ability to obtain desired items is a powerful reinforcer for increased effort at communication. The stimulation of social interaction with an attentive and emotionally engaged caregiver is a second powerful reinforcer of communication for a typically developing youngster. Communication reciprocity develops into a conversation, role-play, joking and humor, problem solving, and interpreting events. Social communication is disrupted for youth on the autism spectrum. At the most basic level, some youth, such as Zoey, fail to develop expressive speech. However, there may also be a communication failure to obtain joint attention with another person through gestures or body language. For otherwise cognitively skillful youth with autism, the normal "serve and return" in conversation may be missing, humor may be misunderstood, and speech phrases may be taken too literally.

3. Adaptive skills for everyday living

Adaptive skills for everyday living and independence refer to taking proper care of bodily needs, such as washing, toileting, dressing, and grooming, or other essentials of self-care, such as brushing teeth and regulating the temperature of a water faucet or eating. Domestic skills fall into this category, including sweeping the floor, wiping down tables and counters, vacuuming, cooking and baking, laundry, and a host of other daily chores necessary for living independently. Some vocational skills include using simple tools, making phone calls, stacking and sorting items, and following a routine in coordination with others in a workspace. Unfortunately, these skills are often below expectations for youth on the autism spectrum. In some cases, this is due to limited intellectual understanding, but for others, it is a lack of appreciation for social or safety consequences.

4. Social and personal leisure and recreational skills

Play characterizes almost all mammals, but particularly humans. Infants seek stimulation by interacting with any item that can be seen, grasped, and mouthed. Play develops in a variety of directions: abstract or imaginary play in which social scenarios are acted out; games in which socially agreed-on rules are followed; athletic play using gross motor skills for running, jumping, tagging, climbing, kicking, and throwing; and individual play in which a child may use materials in solitary exploration or skill development, such as drawing, building, painting, or manipulating. For youth on the severe to moderate ends of the autism spectrum, play's social and imaginary aspects may be completely absent. Recreational pursuits may end up limited to a few repetitive motor or sensory behaviors, typically done alone. For instance, when toys are used, only one aspect of the toy is manipulated, such as spinning a car wheel or repetitively pushing a button to make a sound. Without considerable parenting and therapeutic effort, a child may end up restricted to only a few core "recreational" pursuits.

5. Community integration

The ability to move about in a community, and to be socially and physically safe in the community, is essential to human independence and survival. Some community activities are functional, such as shopping for groceries or visiting a physician. Other activities are recreational or social, such as visiting a park or a movie theater. Lack of safety awareness, such as crossing a street safely, can be a serious hazard for youth on the autism spectrum, limiting their eventual independence. However, negative social consequences are also a barrier to community functioning. For example, if a child takes food from the plates of neighboring diners or screams and talks loudly in a theater, or makes rude comments to passersby, the social consequences can range from embarrassing to dangerous.

Application of the five treatment parameters to Zoey

 Sitting at his desk in a room with five other students, Zoey alternated his focus between rubbing his hands and looking at items on his desk. He looked around the room and repeated this sequence until his teacher said, "Zoey, it's time to work," and pulled out some baskets and colored dice to practice categorization. Zoey's facial expression immediately transformed from cheerful to worried. He shook his head, pressed his hands together, and loudly proclaimed, "Ah, ah." The body language was clear: he was unhappy about this. Usually allowed to choose a picture icon representing something he would be willing to work for, he did not do so on this occasion. Finally, his teacher held out some cubes and suggested, "You can work for a break." Zoey sat back, leaning against the wall, looking up at her, shaking his head a few times, but he finally started the task, sorting the cubes by color. Between bursts of quick sorting, he would clap, smell his fingers, and press them together in a repetitive pattern.

Zoey was required to complete four academic or vocational jobs before earning his break. A "dollar" placed on a chart represented the completion of each task. Four dollars could be cashed in for special snacks, toys, or a break time. Zoey matched colors and shapes (cognitive task) and put small lids on canisters (fine-motor vocational skill) before cashing in his dollars for his break, counting them out to the therapist (a social and math skill).

Theraplay time started. With his teacher sitting next to him, Zoey was helped to make painted hand prints and designs on a large white page. Zoey was assisted through washing his hands with soap and water, receiving physical support and prompting from the therapist. Zoey, his teacher, and the therapist then transitioned into face-to-face partner activities. While Zoey and his teacher had a leg tied together for a three-legged walk, Zoey looked questioningly into his teacher's eyes, making a strong eye gaze and pointing downward. She interpreted his unspoken question, saying, "Look at that! What is he [the therapist] doing?" Coordinating his movement with his teacher, Zoey walked back and forth across the room. Next, Zoey and his teacher required more conscious cooperation to remove the leg bandana, holding a balloon between their shoulders while walking. Then the therapist, teacher, and Zoey took turns hitting or kicking the balloon from person to person in a circle. Once Zoey clearly understood the principle of alternating between partners, a real soccer ball was pulled out. Zoey tried to pick it up and throw it like a balloon, but, with a few demonstrations, then kicked it back and forth. When his attention wandered, the therapist put his arm around Zoey's shoulders and helped him kick the ball to his teacher in the "goal zone." The therapist and teacher cheered enthusiastically for his accurate kicks, eliciting big smiles from Zoey.

The following five therapeutic principles were applied with Zoey:

1. Theraplay application to social interaction and relationships skills

Moving Zoey from completely isolated, independent, and repetitive play to social play, sharing, and turn-taking was a key element behind the Theraplay activities chosen for him. Lack of social attention to another person was a barrier. Lacking a sense of coordinating his body, goals, and intentions with another person was addressed by starting with Zoey and his teacher with their legs physically tied together. The surprise of being physically attached to his teacher during the three-legged walk strongly aroused his attention, prompting some non-verbal social language, which his teacher was able to interpret and respond to. Zoey then had to coordinate with his teacher in his movements to cross the room with her. Experiencing success, combined with enthusiasm from his teacher and therapist, promoted additional cooperation. Zoey was willing to try other games involving other body coordination and goals with another person.

Social reciprocity and sharing were facilitated by turn-taking in hitting a balloon in a circle and kicking a ball back and forth with another person. Intrinsic motivation was maintained by intense shouts of enthusiasm from the teacher and therapist, physical touch, and a rapid pace of activity. Attunement to Zoey's emotional responses, attentional focus, comprehension, and personal enthusiasm was necessary to regulate the intensity level of the activity and to know how much support or instruction to provide. The therapist and teacher used Zoey's non-verbal communication as his speech, commenting on his facial cues and gestures, thus modeling social communication for him.

2. Behavior Therapy and Theraplay application to social communication skills

Asking for something you want is repeatedly encouraged throughout instructional tasks. Lack of awareness that someone's attention needs to be commanded before communicating is a weakness for many people on the severe end of the autism spectrum, especially when cognitive delays are present. Through repeated practice, Zoey was taught to use the Picture Exchange Communication System, or PECS (Frost & Bondy 2002). During the initial phases of training, Zoey was offered something of high personal interest, and then physically prompted to use a picture of the item to ask for it. Later, the prompt could be a more natural gesture from the communicative partner (e.g., a hands-wide shrug with a questioning facial expression) or a specific question (e.g., "What do you want?"). With practice, Zoey learned to get the communicative partner's attention by grunting, touching them, or taking their hand, and then putting the picture in the person's hand. The teacher might ask, "Zoey, what do you want to work for during school work time?" He could reply by handing over an icon representing an item or activity (e.g., snack, toy, break) that would motivate him.

The teacher and therapist modeled listening and commenting. Modeling occurred in multiple ways. When handed an icon, they would recite aloud the communicated intent, such as "I want a break, please." Then they would interpret Zoey's non-verbal social language. For instance, when Zoey looked questioningly at his teacher while the therapist attached their legs with a bandana, the teacher said to him, "Look at that! What is he doing?" In addition, by touching his hand, she used a tone of voice that also promoted emotional regulation, showing attunement to the possibility that Zoey might feel uncertain about this new situation. In other situations, she might promote verbal expressions of empathy, such as "You are not too sure about that; you might feel a little worried."

3. Behavior Therapy application to adaptive skills for everyday living

Skills for everyday living need to be practiced frequently and across many different environments to ensure that skill use is generalized from one situation or setting to another. Washing hands is not only for after using the restroom or before a meal, but can be done whenever your hands are dirty. Thus, the finger painting activity was included, in part, because it created an opportunity for Zoey to recognize a need, decide how to resolve it appropriately (wash rather than wipe hands on clothing), and properly sequence through the steps of cleaning his hands. The teacher and therapist assisted in ensuring that Zoey did it correctly at first. Since verbal explanations afterward would be hard for Zoey to understand, the teacher and therapist prompted him through handwashing each step of the way, using a combination of verbal, gestural, and physical prompts, depending on the need. Over time, the prompts faded as he showed reliability with improved skills.

School activities included those directly applicable to either life functioning or future vocational tasks. Sorting items by color, shape, and type applies to such domestic tasks as sorting clothes and putting away eating utensils. Putting lids on jars applies to developing the fine-motor skill and knowledge for putting away food at home or assisting with a packaging job in a work setting.

4. Theraplay application to leisure and recreational skills

A meaningful and healthy life (physically and mentally) generally requires the ability to engage in a range of leisure or recreational activities. Social engagement is a large part of this, doing activities with another person or a group. Having a repertoire of activities you can do by yourself and a repertoire you can do with others is essential. While people on the spectrum may feel content with only one or two preferred activities and few social interactions, a limited repertoire of social and personal recreational skills can limit their own life and the lives of others. Zoey initially presented with very few social play skills, making it hard for others to have a satisfying relationship with him. His generally limited communication resulted in social isolation from peers, extended family, and even nuclear family members. Cousins, aunts, and uncles struggled to relate to him; some eventually avoided him altogether. Zoey enjoyed eating at restaurants and swimming, but the expense of eating out and the specialized conditions for swimming (such as ready access to a swimming pool at times he could go with his mother) limited the enjoyment of a social relationship with even nuclear family members. Limited social engagement combined with challenging behavior and little educational programming resulted in Zoey living in our residential program; the probability was high that he would never live at home again.

Within the Theraplay sessions with Zoey, we focused on social capacities, such as sharing, turn-taking, and cooperation, as well as on expanding his skills in playing different games or using various materials. In the context of high structure, familiar and trusted educational staff, and high enthusiasm and encouragement, Zoey quickly developed interest and skills in a variety of new activities: these were ball and balloon play, making rhythms with sound instruments, exploring light-up and vibration sensory toys with another person, popping bubbles, kicking a soccer ball, and finger painting, among others.

Zoey's mother had taken early childhood special education classes to understand her son better and consider a career change. She was highly motivated to enhance Zoey's life and their ability to have a relationship together. Video-recorded Marschak Interaction Method (MIM) assessment showed high motivation and effort on her part, but severe limitations due to Zoey's restricted repertoire and pressure to conform to the expected routine of activities. Once Zoey had developed new skills and interests through individual therapy, his shared social experience with his mother quickly improved. Through practice and video feedback, she used what we had practiced with Zoey in her activities at home. Zoey and his mother rapidly grew in their socially shared experience, finding many new meaningful things to do together. These included many of the activities he had learned to enjoy in Theraplay sessions (balloon games, kicking a soccer ball, bean bag tossing games, playing catch, painting, and exploring sensory objects). Zoey also developed some additional ability for individual leisure. The expanded repertoire helped him connect with extended family, making social events more enjoyable for everyone, and giving Zoey's cousins a greater appreciation for him.

5. Behavior Therapy application for community integration

Social skills must be practiced across various situations and people to be truly useful for expanding a person's life options and functioning. Greetings, regulated behavior, and communication must be used outside the therapist's office, home, school, or residential program. To have a social life that involves community outings with family, appropriate behavior must be demonstrated in stores, restaurants, parks, and theaters. Earning money requires demonstrating vocational skills, social skills, and controlled behavior in a work setting. While these statements may sound obvious, many youth on the autism spectrum fail to generalize their skills outside of the people or environments where they learned them. Greetings may be used only with specific teachers or aides. Picture communication might be used only for snacks within a particular classroom. Controlled behavior practiced with a therapist may not be used when wanting access to a favorite toy at home or in a store.

Picture communication with Zoey was immediately practiced with various communication partners (teachers, staff, therapists) and for various desires (food, toys, activities, using the restroom, etc.). He was then taken on trips in the community and encouraged to use his communication skills in restaurants or other public places. Zoey's mother encouraged play and leisure skills by trying out different activities across settings or by including additional people when available. Appropriate social behavior, such as being quiet and calm while watching a movie, or waiting in line after selecting an item for purchase, was practiced in school or in the residential unit, and then on staff-supported outings to real community establishments. Sometimes arrangements were made with work sites, stores, or recreational places to have youth come and practice. Still, the goal was always working up to appropriate behavior and skill use in typical conditions with other shoppers and expected contingencies. Zoey proved adept at developing these skills when provided with support and guidance and the clearly established rules of a setting. For instance, he learned to spend time in a store, select items, stand in line at a checkout, and give the clerk money. He could walk around a museum, using gestures to point things out that interested him.

Conclusion

Theraplay and behavior therapy interventions were integrated with the educational programming of communication and daily life skill programming with recreational enhancement and community activities. Zoey showed tremendous gains in all areas, accompanied by increased social relationship and leisure skills with his mother. Eventually, to everyone's surprise, he was able to return home and live with his mother. The integration of Theraplay and Applied Behavior Analysis (ABA) with behavior therapy made this possible. Principles of ABA were used to teach basic communication skills. The enhanced repertoire of enjoyed recreational activities with Zoey's mother gave them meaningful things to communicate. Positive reinforcement systems were implemented to motivate Zoey to participate in educational and vocational training activities. At the same time, the social engagement activities of Theraplay gave Zoey social and emotional capacities to participate in cooperative social activities, respond with emotional connection, and enjoy mutual attention to a shared activity with others. Progress in all five treatment parameters was necessary for Zoey to live at home successfully. These five domains remain the backbone of therapy for youth with serious cognitive and life skill limitations.

Chapter 5

Integrating Multiple Systems of Therapy

Both Zoey and Geoffrey had difficulties across many life domains. Both had minimal verbal expression. Verbal communication was limited to predominantly emotionally expressed sounds, which they would combine with gestures to indicate what they wanted or if they were asking for something. Their thinking tended to be very concrete, which meant it was hard to explain the reasons for learning a new skill or for a schedule change. They could wander heedlessly into a street or parking lot, showing no regard for traffic. Since a car had never hit them, their understanding of this danger was non-existent. By age 20, no amount of explanation had made any difference in their traffic safety behavior. However, they had learned to habitually wait near a member of staff before proceeding away from a vehicle. Any self-care, safety, or domestic chore skills had to be learned through repeated rote practice, embedded in their daily routine. A caregiving staff or teacher would demonstrate a skill, then use hand-over-hand guidance to assist them through the task.

No single therapy will ever be adequate for children and youth who have life skill difficulties across many domains. This argument may seem obvious, but consider how the medical or therapy model often works. For example, a child has an infection and is taken to the physician (single provider), who prescribes an antibiotic for the cure (single treatment). Another child who suffers a phobia of dogs is taken to a cognitive therapist (single provider), who applies a systematic desensitization program (single treatment) for the cure. A cultural mindset develops that mental health problems are singular events and that a singular therapy treats the issue. If one therapy fails to produce a result, it may be the wrong one and should be changed. Research is then generated to compare singular treatments for singular problems. When confronted with a child with complex developmental difficulties, the absurdity of the model quickly becomes apparent. There is no one behavior therapy, occupational therapy, teaching program, or social skills group that will resolve the entirety of the problem. Only an integrated and comprehensive approach will be beneficial.

A successful system of therapies for children and youth on the autism spectrum will typically include occupational therapy, speech therapy, special education supports, social skills groups, and behavior therapy, among others. Theraplay integrates well with all of them because of its emphasis on social relationships and developmental-sensory play.

Behavior therapy is commonly integrated throughout a therapeutic and educational program. It is based on principles of reward, conditioning, modeling, and learning. These are well-established rules for how humans operate and gain motivation, rules that all humans operate by, including positive and negative reinforcement and avoidance of aversive experiences. In addition, it includes the development of habits through repetition, vicarious learning through watching others, and conditioned responses to specific sensory experiences. Understanding these basic principles is valuable for any therapist, as they can be integrated with any type of therapy or educational program.

Key concepts

- *Positive reinforcer:* Any object, activity, or experience that the individual finds desirable or enjoyable increases the likelihood they will engage in a behavior an increasing amount to obtain it. For example, if a child enjoys winning gymnastic medals, they may increase practice sessions in order to obtain more medals.

- *Negative reinforcer:* Any object, activity, or experience that the individual finds undesirable or unpleasant increases the likelihood they will engage in a behavior to remove it. For example, if a person with chronic headaches discovers aspirin removes headache pain, they will be motivated to use aspirin more often.

- *Extrinsic reinforcer:* Tangible objects or activities an individual can obtain outside of themselves that motivate them to engage in some behavior to get them, including toys, tokens, food, videos, money, clothing, etc. Most items in this category are enjoyed in the short term, and the person is easily satiated with them. However, they can be easy to control and define.

- *Intrinsic reinforcer:* Internal experiences relative to personal beliefs, self-generated thoughts, or attachment and relationship connection. These are very powerful and sustained over time when strong. For example, a person who enjoys the experience of speed may seek skiing experiences throughout their lifetime.

- *Task analysis:* This is the process of breaking a task down into small component steps, each of which can be taught step-wise. Youth on the autism spectrum, especially with developmental delay, often need tasks taught in small parts, done the same way each time. For example, washing hands requires multiple steps, best taught with high structure and a focus on each part:

1. Turn on the water.

2. Run hands under the water.

3. Obtain soap.

4. Rub hands together to create lather.

5. Rinse hands under the water.

6. Turn off the water.

7. Obtain a towel.

8. Dry hands.

9. Throw away paper towels or rehang cloth towels.

- *Chain of behavior:* Most activities require a series of steps, one leading to the next. For instance, driving a car requires obtaining keys, opening the door, sitting inside the car, starting the car, putting the car in drive, checking the blind spots, and so on. We develop a habitual set of behaviors that are performed each time in the service of the total activity. One step in the chain becomes the cue or prompt to do the subsequent step.

- *Habitual sequences:* Some activities become so routine that we do them almost automatically without considering rewards. For instance, when we sit to eat, we typically use our utensils the same way every time. There is no need for thought, prompting, or rewards.

Applied Behavior Analysis

Applied Behavior Analysis (ABA) is the term for methods of studying what motivates a person and what may be interfering with success. A deep understanding of ABA can provide powerful insights for improving a person's life, but when misunderstood or inadequately used, it can have damaging effects.

 For instance, resident Sean, a 16-year-old youth on the autism spectrum, frequently threw himself down to repeatedly bang his head on the floor. Unable to explain his reasoning for this due to limited verbal skills, his actions seemed to occur randomly. Medication changes had no effect, no medical problems were diagnosed, and no correlation was observed with specific daily times or activities. A structured set of behavioral experiments was conducted as a functional behavioral assessment (FBA). Under very controlled and video-recorded conditions, it was observed that Sean tolerated challenging tasks, reprimands, and giving up items or activities of interest. However, he was highly dependent on having frequent and encouraging social interaction. Head banging was almost exclusively tied to having more than ten minutes pass by without personal social interaction. The intervention was then apparent—give Sean personal social interaction and encouragement every 5–10 minutes. When this protocol was followed, the dangerous head-banging behavior completely abated.

The very beneficial outcome for Sean can be contrasted with the harmful effects for Joe due to poorly applied ABA principles. Joe, ten years old, was a child adopted from a neglectful situation and dependent on social support. He could erupt in anger in the middle of a class due to frustration over simple math or reading problems. It was necessary to have a 1:1 assistant in the class to provide prompting and help. Sometimes this was still inadequate, and he could throw tantrums that were hazardous to his classmates. At the end of an FBA, a behavior therapist concluded that "Joe engaged in tantrum behavior for attention." The recommendation was to deprive Joe of attention when he became disruptive, expressly by isolating him in a small room alone. Sadly, the school complied, not realizing that this replicated the rejection, isolation, and confinement of his prior abusive settings, and the consequence was worsened behavior and prolonged tantrums with self-injurious behavior.

The latter behavior therapist clearly lacked a deeper understanding of critical mental health principles or issues related to conditioning and trauma. A separate therapist with both ABA and attachment training explained that of course Joe's behavior was done for attention, but the answer was not a removal of all attention. Instead, the intervention in such a situation was to provide attention in the form of emotional support, reducing task demands when Joe was frustrated, teaching coping skills, and enhancing his social-emotional security. ABA and its associated approaches can be exceptionally powerful in promoting change and new learning. Still, a comprehensive and compassionate understanding of the person must be part of the process.

One of the drawbacks to the way ABA principles are often taught and applied is the excessive focus on external rewards and punishments or consequences, ignoring the neurological and relationship-attachment factors. An external or extrinsic reward is some tangible object or activity outside of yourself that you work for. An intrinsic reward is an internal, emotionally based reward within yourself. To appreciate the difference, consider how far you would run or how much pain you would endure if merely paid for it in money. Then consider how much more you would dedicate to the effort if it were to save the life of a loved one. The internal drive to connect with and benefit loved ones purely for the joy of the relationship is among the most potent and enduring types of motivation. In our experience, there has been a tendency of ABA therapists to overlook these intrinsic factors.

A second drawback to ABA approaches sometimes occurs when teaching social skills. The social skill may be learned and used rotely, poorly integrated with the meaning and purpose of the action. A social skill such as shaking hands may be performed without the sense of appropriate timing, social decorum, or purpose of meaning it has for a typically social person. Attentiveness to social context is vital in the social skills training process, which is a strength in the Theraplay system, and is becoming more acknowledged in the realm of behavior therapy.

ABA is exceptionally useful for clarifying a child's needs and setting up a motivational plan.

 For example, first grader Jose struggled with reading and was required to participate in specialized reading instruction, which he found tiresome and difficult. It was hard to keep his attention on the task long enough to ensure that instructional material was being absorbed. However, Jose also adored remote-controlled trucks. His reading participation was dramatically increased by setting up an agreement that truck play would be a reward for completing a specified number of exercises.

There is more to it than just motivation, however. Adaptive skills for everyday living can be very effectively taught using structured and concrete teaching methods based on ABA principles. Habitual practice leads to sustained behavioral chains, which are addressed further in Chapter 7.

Conclusion

Each concept has a science of learning and teaching associated with it. These behavioral methods are some of the most researched topics in the behavioral science world. Applications of ABA and behavioral approaches to therapy or making life changes are innumerable. We believe that any other therapeutic modality can be enhanced if these behavioral principles are integrated in a skillful manner.

Chapter 6

The Joint Attention Observational Coding System in the Marschak Interaction Method

Widely recognized developmental milestones involve achievements in using complex social engagement skills to interact and respond to others, rooted in caregiver–child interaction. The Marschak Interaction Method (MIM) is such a clinical tool designed to observe and explore the quality of the caregiver–child interaction in a structured way. The MIM consists of a series of play-based tasks to assess dyadic interactions between caregiver and child by evaluating the caregiver's capacities and the child's responses in the four Theraplay dimensions of structure, engagement, nurture, and challenge. The results of the MIM guide therapists to develop Theraplay treatments to address problem areas in the relationship effectively. Since its inception, MIM has been an essential observational assessment tool for many Theraplay therapists and play therapists to determine healthy dyadic patterns between caregiver and child. It has also been taught in family therapy programs as a method of family assessment, as many therapists have testified to the power of the current MIM analysis system in guiding Theraplay treatment planning for enhancing the relationship between caregiver and child.

When conducting MIM with children on the autism spectrum, therapists quickly encounter difficulty in measuring the quality of caregiver–child interaction due to the interference of autistic features that are intertwined and emerge concurrently in the exchanges. Considering the variability in levels of functioning and a broad range of symptomology among children on the autism spectrum, it is a natural inclination for therapists to attempt to understand the strengths and vulnerabilities in child development during the MIM administration. In addition, some caregivers of children on the autism spectrum tend to expect more than enhanced caregiver–child relationships, and focus on how Theraplay may help their children gain skills to function better in society. It is often helpful when therapists and caregivers discuss the impact of Theraplay on the social-emotional capacities of children. Assessing additional areas of children's social-emotional capacities in the MIM will be useful to effectively educate caregivers about Theraplay to best meet their child's needs.

The MIM offers excellent opportunities to understand the levels of social-emotional capacities of children on the autism spectrum. Moreover, since autistic behaviors are observable, Theraplay therapists benefit from quantifying clinical observations, if specific guidelines exist. In 2018, Hiles Howard *et al.* (2018) used an adapted five-point Likert scoring system for MIM interactions in 16 dimensions (six for the parent; seven for the child; three for the dyad), which can be categorized into ten domains: (1) observed facial expression (child, parent); (2) positive or negative vocalization towards the other (child, parent); (3) proximity of the body oriented towards the other (child, parent); (4) responsivity of the other's affective or behavioral cues (child, parent); (5) maintained or deviated eye gaze (child, parent); (6) guidance (parent–give, child–accept); (7) task focus (child only); (8) engaged or disengaged social interactions (dyad); (9) balance of initiating and controlling behaviors (dyad); and (10) overall impression of quality interactions (dyad). By scoring each dimension of the MIM, the researchers identified the effectiveness of a two-week intensive Theraplay intervention in improving areas of affect, joint attention, and social cooperation in parents and children on the autism spectrum (Hiles Howard *et al.* 2018). Adapting from this study and other validated scales for children on the autism spectrum, we explore an additional domain that seems suitable for understanding the social and emotional functioning of children on the autism spectrum, which is joint attention.

Joint attention

Joint attention is defined as signaling and responding mutually with expressions, sounds, and gestures (Adamson *et al.* 2012; Jones & Carr 2004; Kasari *et al.* 2010; Wetherby & Woods 2006). Children on the autism spectrum have difficulty initiating joint attention with others, often evident before the first year of life (Jones & Carr 2004). They struggle with forming joint attention with others using gestures and eye gazes and responding to bids for joint attention from others. Deficits in joint attention recursively keep children on the autism spectrum from getting enough responses from caregivers because parental responses tend to be determined by their children's initiations (Ruble *et al.* 2008; Tamis-LeMonda, Bornstein, & Baumwell 2001). In addition, caregivers are unsure how to initiate joint attention with their child on the autism spectrum due to their child's restricted interests in play or social engagement. Given that synchronizing caregivers' verbal and non-verbal responses to their child on the autism spectrum improves their social communication development (Aldred, Green, & Adams 2004), we must explore ways of strengthening parental responses to children on the autism spectrum. Fortunately, Theraplay is a powerful method for creating attuned engagement between caregiver and child, an essential quality for increasing synchrony and reciprocal responses that contribute to the social and emotional capacities of children on the autism spectrum.

Since structured and engagement-based assessment helps increase caregivers' play and engagement (Gutierrez *et al.*, 2013; Hagopian *et al.*, 2004), measuring joint attention in MIM will help therapists and caregivers monitor the progress of children on the autism spectrum and deliver effective Theraplay treatment. Given that the validity of usefulness in the current MIM analysis offers sufficient guidance to understand the dyad between caregiver and child, we suggest supplementing the joint attention coding system in MIM for children on the autism spectrum.

Defining the sub-domains of joint attention

We first develop a clear understanding of joint attention in the Joint Attention Observation Coding System (JAOCS; see Appendix 2) based on collective information from the DSM-5 (*Diagnostic and Statistical Manual of Mental Disorders, 5th edn*; APA 2013) diagnostic criteria for social-communication deficits and research in joint attention and identified sub-domains in joint attention: non-verbal affect, verbal affect, initiation, responses, eye gaze, and mirroring (see Table 6.1).

Table 6.1. Joint attention behavior terminology

Term	Definition	Example for Yes (Y)	Example for No (N)
Non-verbal affect	Positive or negative facial affect expressions, such as smiles, laughs, frowns, yelling, screams, etc.	The child frowns by turning his head when Mom takes squeaky animals (pigs) from the envelope	The child is not aware of his mom's actions and continues to be preoccupied with what he has been doing
Verbal affect	Verbal statements or expressions of positive, negative, or neutral affect toward the mother	The child shouts out "Pig!" when Mom takes squeaky animals from the envelope	The child says "Snack" when Mom takes squeaky animals (pigs) from the envelope
Initiation	Verbal or non-verbal initiating behavior with parents using appropriate sounds, speech, expressions, and gestures	The child squeezes and jumps his pig, saying "Oink" as soon as Mom takes it from the envelope	The child jumps around the room when Mom says "Come here, let's play with pigs"
Responses	Verbal or non-verbal responding behaviors using appropriate sounds, speech, expressions, and gestures	When Mom says "I am going to tag you," the child quickly moves his pig to jump	The child has no response when Mom says, "I am going to tag you"
Eye gaze	Intentionally looking at the parent's eyes	The child looks at Mom's eyes when Mom says "It's fun" during play	The child does not make any eye contact
Mirroring	Copying the parent's non-verbal or verbal initiations or responses without prompts	When Mom squeezes her pig, the child starts squeezing his pig	The child does not copy any of his mom's actions or repeat Mom's words

Then we develop an observational assessment method adapting a technique in momentary time sampling (MTS; Cooper, Heron, & Heward 2007). MTS is chosen because this method allows us to concurrently measure six sub-domains (in other words, six observable behaviors) in joint attention quantitatively.

Procedure

We recommend measuring six behaviors (non-verbal affect, verbal affect, initiation, response, eye gaze, and mirroring) for ten minutes in total during the MIM (six minutes from engagement-based activity, three minutes from challenge-based activity, and one minute from nurture-based activity). The rationale for measuring more engagement and challenge activities in JAOCS is that those activities tend to have a more interactive nature during caregiver–child play.

To collect accurate data on joint attention, we divide the total observation time into 30-second intervals (see Table 6.2). Suppose a child manifests joint attention items when the timer reaches the 30-second marker—record "Y" in each item for that interval. For instance, if a child manifests all six items for 30 seconds during play with squeaky animals, the total joint attention score for the first 30 seconds will be 6 points. Hypothetically, a child's maximum score will be 120 points if each item's whole point (12 points in one minute) is earned during ten minutes. The total obtained joint attention score in the MIM will be a baseline, and therapists can monitor the score in Theraplay sessions (six minutes in engagement-based activities; three minutes for a challenge-based activity; and one minute for a nurture-based activity) and the post-MIM. Also, if a child is described as having severe autistic behavior, a therapist may decide to use one-minute intervals to collect data during a 15-minute MIM session.

Further, it is essential to consider the following recommendations when administering the joint attention observational coding system in MIM:

- The first 1–2 minutes of the squeaky animals task is a warm-up period for the caregiver and child to become used to this task. Start coding after a warm-up period.

- Start coding after a caregiver reads the task instructions. Once you start a timer, use a consistent three minutes or one minute (feeding) with a 30-second interval to code each item in tasks.

- Mark "Y" once, regardless of the frequency of the behavior. For instance, if a child shows a specific behavior multiple times during one interval (e.g., smiles at Mom most of the time in a 0–30-second interval), mark "Y" once. Then note the quality of the targeted behavior ("smiles" in this example) in the observational summary section.

 Alex is four years old. He is the oldest of two children and resides with both parents. He has attended an Advanced Behavior Analysis (ABA) program since he was diagnosed with being on the autism spectrum at age three. Linda (Alex's mom) contacted this particular therapist because she had not seen any progress in Alex's autistic behavior. Furthermore, she felt that Alex had decreased interest in playing with toys. The MIM administration results yielded that Linda's strengths were engagement and nurture. However, it was challenging to see shared joy, reciprocity, and synchrony in their interactions because Alex showed no interest in completing the tasks. In addition, he did not reciprocate when his mom attempted to engage with him through play or conversation. Using a video-taped MIM session, we coded joint attention using a 30-second interval for ten minutes (see Table 6.3).

Alex scored 29 points out of 120 for joint attention in the pre-Therapy MIM. Alex joined 20 weekly Theraplay treatments (two pre-post MIM, three parent feedback sessions, 15 Theraplay sessions) with his mom while reducing the ABA program from 20 hours to ten. In addition, Linda was assigned 15-minute daily home Theraplay activities focusing on the engagement aspect. Six sessions (pre-Therapy MIM, four Theraplay sessions, and post-Therapy MIM) were video-recorded to monitor the progress of Alex's joint attention ability. His joint attention increased from 29 points to 49 points, yielding a 59.1% increase (see Figure 6.1).

Table 6.2. Sample form for collecting the joint attention score

Task (seconds)	Non-verbal affect		Verbal affect		Initiation		Responses		Eye gaze		Mirroring		Total # of Y
0–30	Y	N	Y	N	Y	N	Y	N	Y	N	Y	N	
31–60	Y	N	Y	N	Y	N	Y	N	Y	N	Y	N	
61–90	Y	N	Y	N	Y	N	Y	N	Y	N	Y	N	
91–120	Y	N	Y	N	Y	N	Y	N	Y	N	Y	N	
121–150	Y	N	Y	N	Y	N	Y	N	Y	N	Y	N	
151–180	Y	N	Y	N	Y	N	Y	N	Y	N	Y	N	
3 minutes	# of Y:		# of Y:		# of Y:		# of Y:		# of Y:		# of Y:		# of Y:
Observational summary													

Note: Y = yes and N = no.

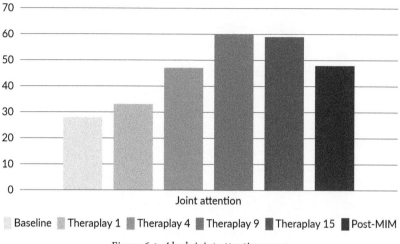

Figure 6.1. Alex's joint attention score

The results matched parental reports of Alex's increased responses to parental initiations. Among the items in joint attention, the most change was in "Responses" (4 responses to 10), and "Mirroring" made the least (0 to 2 mirroring), shown in Figure 6.2.

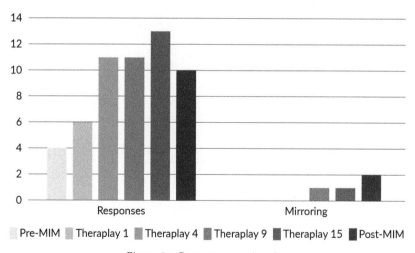

Figure 6.2. Responses vs. mirroring

The joint attention observational coding system in MIM was helpful for Linda to specify the progress of Alex's positive changes, and motivated her to continue Theraplay-based interactions.

Table 6.3. Pre-therapy MIM joint attention coding system results for Alex

Task: Squeaky animals (seconds)	Non-verbal affect		Verbal affect		Initiation		Responses		Eye gaze		Mirroring		Total # of Y
0–30	☒	N	Y	N	Y	N	☒	N	Y	N	Y	N	2
31–60	☒	N	Y	N	Y	N	Y	N	Y	N	Y	N	1
61–90	Y	N	☒	N	Y	N	Y	N	☒	N	Y	N	2
91–120	☒	N	Y	N	☒	N	Y	N	Y	N	Y	N	2
121–150	☒	N	Y	N	Y	N	Y	N	Y	N	Y	N	1
151–180	☒	N	Y	N	Y	N	Y	N	Y	N	Y	N	1
3 minutes	5		1		1		1		1		0		9
Observational summary	Alex mostly shows non-verbal affect by smiling and laughing. However, he constantly squeezes the pig next to his ear, as if he seeks auditory stimuli. He once responded to his mom's pig with a good eye gaze when she pounded her pig on his pig several times.												

Task: Familiar games (seconds)	Non-verbal affect	Verbal affect	Initiation	Responses	Eye gaze	Mirroring	Total # of Y
0–30	Y	Y	N	N	N	N	2
31–60	N	N	N	N	N	N	0
61–90	N	N	N	N	N	N	0
91–120	N	N	N	N	N	N	0
121–150	Y	N	N	Y	N	N	2
151–180	Y	N	N	N	N	N	1
3 minutes	3	1	0	1	0	0	5
Observational summary	Linda appears unsure what to play in time. She tickles Alex at first, which elicits his non-verbal affect (smile) and verbal affect (saying "stop"), but it was soon stopped. When Linda asks Alex what to play, Alex starts running around the room. When Linda chases him, Alex responds to her by running faster, with waves of laughter.						

Task: Putting hats on each other (seconds)	Non-verbal affect		Verbal affect		Initiation		Responses		Eye gaze		Mirroring		Total # of Y
0–30	☒	N	☒	N	Y	N	Y	N	Y	N	Y	N	2
31–60	☒	N	Y	N	Y	N	Y	N	Y	N	Y	N	1
61–90	Y	N	☒	N	Y	N	☒	N	Y	N	Y	N	2
91–120	Y	N	Y	N	Y	N	Y	N	Y	N	Y	N	0
121–150	Y	N	Y	N	Y	N	Y	N	Y	N	Y	N	N/O
151–180	Y	N	Y	N	Y	N	Y	N	Y	N	Y	N	N/O
2 minutes	2		2		0		1		0		0		5
Observational summary	When Linda puts a hat on Alex, Alex says, "no," with an annoyed face. Alex refuses to put a hat on his mom, but does it when she says he will get a snack if he does. He presents negative non-verbal affect (frowning face) and negative verbal affect ("no"). The task ends quickly, so only two minutes of coding are made. Note: N/O = no opportunity.												

Task: Feeding (seconds)	Non-verbal affect	Verbal affect	Initiation	Responses	Eye gaze	Mirroring	Total # of Y
0–30	☒ N	☒ N	Y N	☒ N	Y N	Y N	3
31–60	☒ N	Y N	Y N	Y N	☒ N	Y N	2
61–90	☒ N	☒ N	Y N	Y N	☒ N	Y N	3
91–120	☒ N	Y N	☒ N	Y N	Y N	Y N	2
2 minutes	4	2	1	1	2	0	10
Observational summary	Two minutes of coding for feeding are conducted to make a ten-minute MIM coding. Alex was happy to see his favorite snack. He does not feed his mom and eats it alone. He constantly smiles and makes a two-word sentence, "I like." He also shows eye gaze when his mom feeds him.						

Conclusion

There is increasing attention on relationship-focused interventions for children on the autism spectrum (Hiles Howard *et al.* 2018). We are some of the many Theraplay therapists who have firsthand experience in witnessing the positive impact of Theraplay on social and emotional functioning in children on the autism spectrum. Still, objective investigation of joint attention and social engagement in Theraplay has been limited. Thus, the proposed joint attention observational coding system in MIM suggests a potential to fill the current gap. Investigating and refining this system is an ongoing endeavor: for example, we are unaware of the normal range of the joint attention score or what the clinical cutoff is. Certainly, we need extensive validation studies to generalize its use. Although we are at the frontline of this process, we hope that the joint attention observational coding system in MIM provides an opportunity for Theraplay treatments on a continuum of effectiveness, and improves the generalization of child outcomes.

Chapter 7

Structure-Based Interventions

Structured guidance of a child is a core principle within the domains of Theraplay, behavior therapy, and early childhood education. Structure creates a sense of safety for both the child and adults involved: familiar routines and rituals provide a framework for trying new activities and developing skills. In other words, a familiar routine or ritual is an anchor point. Children and youth on the autism spectrum are susceptible to routine and ritual. So much of the social environment is confusing to them, and so much of the sensory world is overwhelming that a schedule, routine, or ritual might provide a sense of safety that they can fall back on to stay calm and grounded. Therefore, the principles of structure within Theraplay, behavior therapy, and early childhood education are highly complementary.

There are seven essential intervention tools for children and youth on the autism spectrum: (1) using a standard schedule; (2) environment and materials management; (3) the Premack principle; (4) task analysis and prompt hierarchy; (5) backward chain teaching; (6) rewards; and (7) generalization of skills to new situations.

1. Scheduling
In Theraplay, entering each therapy session with a clear plan is expected. Sessions typically follow a standard ritual of structured entry to the room, check-in moment between the therapist and child, a series of games that promote the desired relationship skills and rapport, a calm down time, a

period of snack and nurture, a song, and a structured exit. Specific games will change from session to session, but the format remains essentially the same, providing the child with a sense of safe ritual. New things and new challenges can be easier to tolerate in the context of a safe ritual.

It is common in autism support classrooms to use picture schedules to provide structure. The daily and weekly routine remain relatively similar, although specific tasks may change. This may include: (1) a check-in or circle time to review the day and look at the schedule; (2) a series of work tasks; (3) breaks for rest and recreation; (4) a special class (e.g., art, physical education, library time, occupational therapy); (5) meal; (6) clean-up time; and (7) structured exit to go home. The similarity to a Theraplay session is no accident. Specialists in early childhood education and autism largely developed Theraplay. A predictable structure to the day allows more mental energy to be applied to learning.

As part of their Picture Exchange Communication System (PECS), excellent instruction and materials for creating picture schedules to meet autism support needs can be found through Pyramid Educational Consultants.[1] Anyone can use materials at hand to develop schedules that will be meaningful to and understood by children or youth on the autism spectrum who have limited verbal and cognitive skills.

The first step is to list all the activities involved. For therapists, this would include Theraplay games, art activities, or social skill practices, among others. A caregiver list would probably include meals, basic daily skills of brushing teeth and bathing, chores, and community trips. A school-relevant list would include classes, breaks, lunch, special therapies, and field trips.

Once the list of activities is established, the therapist, caregiver, or teacher obtains pictures that strongly depict or symbolize that activity. A Theraplay therapist should have the following pictures at hand: bean bags or beanie animals representing bean bag games, balloons, bubbles, lotion, paint, a drink, a snack, music, ball, swing, etc. Entrance and exit activities may be included to signify the start and end of the session. In contrast, a caregiver might have pictures for getting dressed, breakfast, brushing

---

1   https://pecs.com

teeth, picking up toys, snacks, car trips, grocery shopping, getting on the bus, showering, pajamas, reading books, and many more.

A balance must be struck between visibility and manipulative skills. A square picture approximately 1–2 inches is commonly used, with sticky material placed on the back. Hook and loop tape (or Velcro) is a popular choice. Hook tape can be placed on the back of the picture cards, and latch tape on a piece of cardboard, plastic binder, clipboard, or wall. This is now a durable, reusable schedule system.

Therapists may introduce a schedule in the waiting room or immediately on entering the therapy office. This sets up an expectation and routine the child can use for feeling grounded, helping them understand what will happen in the therapy and when it will be done. Knowing when to expect an ending is important. If the child dislikes some activities, they can use the schedule to see that it will be over soon and that some possibly preferable activity will take the place of the opposed activities, or appreciate that it will end quickly. Knowing that the ending is coming sets the expectations for finishing up, reducing potential tantrums over terminating a preferred activity if the child has a strong positive response and is enjoying activities. The schedule often takes on a life and authority of its own, so a child can blame the schedule for a transition or ending rather than the therapist. The schedule sets the rule.

A Theraplay therapist's schedule might look something like this:

Entrance
Check for hurts
Balloon games
Toy car push
Bubble pop
Paint roller
Blanket swing
Snack
Snuggle with Dad
Exit

Many children are helped by taking the picture off after each task is done, and then putting it away in an envelope or placing it on a different "Done" card. As children become comfortable with the routine, removing items may be unnecessary—just visually referencing the schedule may be adequate. At the end of the session, a special snack and snuggle time with a caregiver capitalizes on the Premack principle. The child is more motivated and cooperative with less preferred activities by knowing that a highly preferred activity is coming soon.

2. Environment and materials management

Behavior therapy and Theraplay both place a strong emphasis on managing the environment. From its initial conception by DesLauriers and Carlson (1969), a fundamental principle was for the therapist to make themself the most interesting and inviting positive reinforcer in the child's environment. The behavioral principle applied is to remove competing reinforcers and distractions. In practical terms, first, this means removing many of the toys or other distractions in the room from sight. Second, this means controlling the toys and materials the therapist plans to use during the therapy. Third, it means using toys or materials primarily as a vehicle for social interaction, making the social exchange focus on fun and excitement.

When applying the integrated Theraplay–behavior therapy program within a residential or in-home setting, our therapists typically were prepared with a small backpack or carrying case that included the following items:

- squishy balls, light-up balls, and high bounce balls, as these met both the sensory needs and visual interests of children, but could be used for back-and-forth games of catch

- a toy car that could be pushed back and forth on a tile floor between the therapist and child

- noisemakers of different types, such as hand clappers, for engaging in rhythm play, cooperative drumming, and turn-taking

- balloons

- cotton balls

- vibration toy for children who enjoy sensory vibration

- small paint brushes or feathers for sensory feel activities

- lotion

- stickers for turn-taking in placing stickers on matching body parts

- small squeaky toys for children who enjoyed back-and-forth squeak exchanges with the therapist; these could create a non-verbal type of social exchange

- bubbles

- one or two additional sensory objects, such as therapy putty or squeezable non-toxic dough, rubbery animal, bean bag, comb or brush

- small packages of edible snacks.

With this small assortment of objects, there are hundreds of activity permutations involving social interaction sequences. However, the emphasis is always on the social exchange. Some materials might be used to elicit interest, such as a light-up ball, but it can be quickly parlayed into some reciprocal play or sensory interaction. Furthermore, many activities require no materials, such as the walk–run–stop activity, *Row, Row, Row Your Boat* song while holding hands and rocking back and forth, or copying silly faces and sounds.

Therapy can be conducted in almost any location. Some of the best locations have been the least likely, such as stairwells, empty classrooms, and conference rooms. These locations were found to be particularly successful for producing social engagement precisely because they lacked anything inherently interesting to do in them. In the absence of toys, puzzles, books, TVs, or even furniture in some cases, the only thing of interest became the adult in the room and the small bag of items the adult carried in a pack or their pockets. The primary actions of interest were whatever the adult did. Joint attention between children and adults can be easily directed through tone of voice, presenting an activity, or creating a sensory experience. Occasionally, just the acoustics of the space can sometimes be used. For instance, some children used the ringing echo of stairwells to enjoy singing or making sounds with the therapist.

Therapeutic space can be arranged for increased success using these additional techniques:

- A mat, small rug, or blanket on the ground creates visual space. Similar to the carpet squares used for "circle time" seats in preschool classes, a small blanket creates the sensation or impression of a "special spot" in which social engagement occurs.

- A squishy and deep bean bag seat can be used for the child's comfort. Bean bag seats produce a sensation of containing comfort surrounding the child, resulting in them having less impulse to jump up and move away. In addition, extricating from a deep bean bag is slightly harder than rising from a regular chair or the floor, giving the therapist more time to react and less motivation for the child to get up.

- Draping a heavy blanket around the child is comforting for some. Indeed, some children on the autism spectrum enjoy weighted blankets and stay seated and concentrate for longer with a weighted blanket or vest.

- Be prepared to activate every sensory system in some enjoyable or calming way. Visual interest is the easiest for most people to think of (e.g., light-up objects), since humans have a firm reliance on the visual system. Still, activities can be planned for all sensory systems: smell (e.g., smelly stickers or bubbles or lotions); taste (e.g., different-flavored snacks or jelly beans); vibration (e.g., vibrating object); proprioception or balance (e.g., standing on a balance board or balancing together on one foot while holding hands); temperature (e.g., wrapping a hand in foil generates heat); touch–texture (e.g., having items to feel that may be soft, fuzzy, smooth, sticky, gooey); and auditory (e.g., making crunches with food, clapping or whistling, blowing through sound-makers).

Planning to engage across sensory systems increases the likelihood of attentiveness on the part of any child, even a child with cognitive limitations or concentration problems.

3. The Premack principle

All behavior therapists learn the Premack principle in their first class on principles of intervention. The Premack principle is the concept that humans can be motivated to perform a less preferred activity by the anticipated reward of a more preferred activity. When a parent says, "Do your math homework, and then you are allowed to go outside and play," the Premack principle is capitalized. Schedules work more effectively as a motivational tool when certain, more preferred activities come after the less preferred ones.

Once some therapy has been conducted with a child, the therapist will identify which activities and objects are more interesting or preferred by the child. Then, when introducing a new or less preferred or harder activity, the visual schedule can show the more enjoyed activity coming afterward, increasing the child's motivation to participate in something new or challenging.

4. Task analysis and prompt hierarchy

Teaching practical life skills is an essential therapy component for children on the autism spectrum. Teaching and learning skills are an integral component of life for all humans, and specific teaching methods are more effective than others. While many skills are acquired through observation of others without particular teaching (vicarious learning), much of human learning occurs through specific instruction. For example, skills of dressing, cooking, driving, writing, drawing, and repairing broken items are taught relatively systematically, imparted from caregiver or teacher to student through trials of observation, guided practice, corrective feedback, and re-practice.

Unless an instructor has had specific training in teaching methods, there is a tendency toward imparting knowledge to others relatively haphazardly. Neurotypical children and youth will observe and accept feedback of different types and may ask for clarification when needed.

The ability to learn through observation and verbal feedback cannot be relied on for children and youth on the autism spectrum or with cognitive delays. Learning is particularly hard for children and youth who are on the autism spectrum and have cognitive delay. More structured methods become very important for this population, but structured and systematic teaching methods benefit them all.

Teaching methods are a special focus of training for behavior therapists. Teaching from a task analysis is a core method of teaching all types of skills, from self-care to domestic skills to recreational play and social skills. These methods have particular application to Theraplay when assisting a child in learning a new social play skill, or coaching caregivers on being more effective teachers of skills for their children. Teaching from a task analysis involves studying any task to break it down into its component steps. For instance, putting lotion on another person could involve unscrewing a cap, squeezing an appropriate amount of lotion into your palm, rubbing it to warm it up, taking the other person's hand, and massaging the lotion in with broad strokes and appropriate pressure. Applying lotion is a valuable skill for children to learn as a way to show nurture toward another person, but it is hard for many children to do appropriately, whether they are on the autism spectrum or not. Furthermore, you can imagine other steps, such as asking the recipient to remove a watch, roll up a sleeve, or put a cap back on the lotion.

Creating a list of critical steps to follow to accomplish a task ensures that you are intentional about covering each step. Take a moment to consider how many steps there are to brushing your teeth. Write down the number of steps you can think of before reading further. When teaching tooth brushing to youth in a residential unit that specifically served youth on the autism spectrum, our team identified 26 steps. Was this more than you imagined? If so, this is because most people gloss over many of the steps, as the process becomes highly automatic for most people. By scrutinizing the task for all the small steps involved, the team was able to examine which smaller transitions or actions the youth had the most trouble with (such as brushing the inside of the teeth, which requires turning the brush, angling it, and being aware of the inner surface). Special effort or support could then be focused on problem areas. The list also ensured that all components of the process were covered, right down to turning off the water at the end.

Creating a task analysis promotes greater consistency in teaching a skill. For example, when a driving or flight instructor guides driving or flying, they typically instruct the student to perform critical functions the same way every time, to ensure that safety procedures become automatic. After multiple trials, the procedures become an ingrained habit. Similarly, for children, particularly those with cognitive delays, following a task procedure the same way every time increases the learning speed and retention over the long run. You might create a picture flipbook on how to construct a sandwich or cook pancakes. By following the pictured procedure the same way each time, efficiency and long-term retention are maximized.

Learning a task involves more than having a list and a demonstration. The procedure must be performed using motor skills. A simple skill of wiping down a countertop involves obtaining a paper towel and spray, spraying the right amount, and wiping all quadrants of the counter without missing any area. The basic skill of engaging in greetings with a handshake involves multiple steps that include establishing eye contact, verbally greeting, reaching out a hand, grasping the other's hand with the correct pressure, and dropping the hand. Some of these skills are hard to grasp, even for higher-functioning or neurotypical children. Thus, prompting is necessary. Prompting or supporting any person in acquiring a skill ranges from full physical assistance to giving merely a gesture of what to do next.

Behavioral specialists have categorized prompting supports into a hierarchy, as follows:

- full physical support, such as hand-over-hand assistance

- partial physical support, such as physically guiding the other person's hands or arm, spotting for balance, or molding the person into position

- modeling what to do in an explicit manner

- verbal coaching, such as giving a verbal hint or explanation

- gestural prompting, such as a small hand signal to cue the person on what to do next.

Establishing a systematic method of using this hierarchy is important for teaching because independence should be encouraged but undue frustration avoided. People assume a lack of knowledge, motor skills, or observation skills, and push the process too fast, with too little structure or organization. Then the caregiver or teacher becomes annoyed at the child for non-compliance, tantrums, or physical aggression. The goal is to give the optimal amount of scaffolding to accomplish the task and to fade the support gradually as the prompts become unnecessary.

Ideally, start the teaching process with a high amount of physical support, backing off from full physical support to partial physical support for the components of the task the person is showing more skill in. Then, as the skill becomes performed with adequate dexterity, back off from physical prompting to verbal coaching, and from there, fade to small gestural cues to ensure the routine is completed in proper order. When tracking success, a teacher, therapist, or caregiver may document in a chart which type of prompting was supplied (see Appendix 1).

Appendix 1 shows how levels of prompting might be listed in a chart for tracking progress. Multiple columns can be provided for monitoring progress over numerous trials on different days. Teaching in a carefully orchestrated manner with minimal failure and rapid learning is part of the science of behavior therapy. An excellent resource for practical teaching methods, pre-made task analyses, and instructions on prompt hierarchies can be found in the Murdoch Center Program Library and its associated manuals (Wheeler *et al.* 1997). Christine Reeve (2021) has curated additional resources for supporting adaptive skill learning and breaking tasks into manageable components.

Making the learning process fun and rewarding is a crucial element of the Theraplay process. When working on an adaptive skill, be it mopping a floor, washing a car, pulling up weeds, or cleaning a counter, the key concepts are "doing with," creating competence and connection, and positive practice. Children naturally admire adults and their tasks; they aspire to be similar to the adults in their life to whom they feel emotionally connected. Inviting a child to be with their caregiver or teacher while doing a chore with the caregiver or teacher is a powerful opportunity for modeling the skills we want children and older youth to have. It helps if the adult can make a shift in mentality from viewing chores as burdens (negative) to seeing them as mere activities humans do (neutral), or activities that can be fun or meaningful (positive).

5. Backward chain teaching (backward chaining)

Tasks in human society and schools are commonly taught as forwarding chains in which completing one step is the cue to start the next. For example, putting on a shoe is the cue to cross the laces, which is the cue to place one lace under the other and to pull it tight, which is the cue to making a bow. Making bows in the laces is the cue to twist them together and pull the laces tight, which tends to be a difficult task for children to learn. Frustration at any step may result in complaints or tantrum behavior. Many teachers or caregivers have dreamed of having a method in which there is no failure and learning is very reliable. The good news is that behavior therapists have developed such a method. It is called backward chain teaching (backward chaining).

Backward chaining involves teaching or emphasizing the last step first. Imagine teaching a child to wash and put away dishes. Many children are motivated for this task because they see adults do it, and find the bubbles and water fun to interact with. However, children may have been frustrated with the process due to breaking a dish or getting a cut, while many caregivers may have been frustrated with poorly washed dishes. The backward chain teaching method would proceed with the child watching the caregiver turn on the water, put water on the sponge, wet the dish, scrub the dish, dry the dish, and put the dish away. On the second dish, the caregiver would again do everything, but assist the child with putting the dish away, perhaps with full physical support for safety and precision. After some rounds, the caregiver will have faded the support so that the child has done the putting away part independently and competently. Perhaps the next day the caregiver will give full physical support for drying the dish, knowing that the child is competent to put the dish away. Slowly, the support for drying the dish is faded. The caregiver teaches in reverse, supporting the prompt hierarchy, fading as the child demonstrates competence.

In short order, the child will perform the entire dishwashing sequence with high competence, maybe with the adult putting the dishes away at the end. Positive reinforcement in the form of praise is given for success, and the activity also involves social engagement and cooperation between the caregiver and the child, strengthening their relationship. Additional positive reinforcement may occur in adult attention, conversation, music, fun inserted into the task, and a sense of accomplishment for doing something mature. In some cases, a special award may be given in a special ceremony once the child has learned to do an entire sequence of tasks with total independence.

6. Rewards

Positive reinforcement occurs in multiple ways for tasks, some obvious and others less so. Adult attention and presence may be a positive reinforcement for many children when doing a task. For instance, at a supported employment center, a young adult thinks of cleaning a car as a tedious task, but suddenly becomes excited when washing a car in the context of working with a mechanic he admires and gets approval from. Excitement and motivation for this young adult also come from being in an automotive shop learning about car repair and maintenance. Leveraging emotional connection and natural interests as part of the learning process will maximize success over the long run.

Small, frequent rewards are more powerful than big, infrequent rewards. For some tasks or behaviors, a child will require frequent rewards and acknowledgment to stay motivated. It is hard for children on the autism spectrum or with emotional disorders to stay calmly seated, so they experience a major barrier to traveling safely in a car or doing tabletop skills tasks. A program was devised to use random interval reinforcement. An audio recording was played in the background that randomly produced a chime, ranging from two to five minutes. Any child seated when the chime went off would receive a preferred reinforcer. "Preferred reinforcer" means that we had studied what motivated each child. Some children enjoyed M&Ms, and others wanted to collect tokens to cash in, while others might like raisins or something else. Thus, each child received what was meaningful or tasty to them, which was different from some standard reward that any particular child may or may not like—it is only a reinforcer if it is truly motivating. Over time of using this randomizing system of frequent signals and reinforcement, the children shifted toward more seated behavior.

7. Generalization of skills to new situations

Individuals on the autism spectrum typically struggle to generalize a skill or concept from one setting to another. For instance, a child on the autism spectrum who has learned to make a sandwich at school may not think to make one at home if hungry. In our residential program, we commonly noticed that children who had learned to communicate wants in school using picture communication failed to use the communication system in the residential hall or at home. Even in school, they might only communicate with the person who had taught them the system. Intentional efforts were necessary to ensure that skills were transferred or generalized across settings and people.

Skills should be immediately expanded outward to maximize generalization. When training youth in communication, our program emphasized expanding the skills from the first session, from using pictures to communicate with multiple people in the first session alone to walking to another room to communicate a request. Requesting multiple types of items would be practiced. In the same way, our adaptive skills training program would encourage using a skill (e.g., handwashing, wiping down a counter) in multiple situations and locations. Recreational activities—including Theraplay activities—were practiced in multiple settings, including a residential hall, school, gymnasium, community park, and the home.

The family therapy program was heavily oriented toward working on the generalization of all skills: communication, social behavior, and recreational, community, and adaptive tasks. Theraplay activities practiced during individual therapy were also practiced with staff. These social and recreational activities were then practiced with family members who came to sessions that were guided by the therapist. Communication skills were integrated into Theraplay sessions for practice with family members of all types (caregivers, aunts, siblings, grandparents, and family friends). Therapists would accompany the youth on family visits to the home or in the community, where the skills were practiced. Caregivers would be assigned homework to utilize the activities when alone with the child on visits or vacations. In this way, socializing skills, cleaning skills, shopping and community integration activities, recreational and leisure activities, and communication skills were much more rapidly acquired by the youth, and generalized for use across many settings.

Chapter 8

Engagement-Based Interventions

Walking on to the residential unit armed with simple materials, the Theraplay therapist carried out these strange scenes:

- The therapist put a bean bag animal on his head, walked around, and then grasped the hands of the confused and amused youth, counted to three, and dropped the bean bag animal into the hands of the surprised youth, calling out, "Hooray! You caught it," followed by saying, "Now it's *your* turn!" The therapist immediately put the bean bag animal on the youth's head and started counting while holding hands, ready for the drop.

- A balloon was blown to expanded size while gesturing for the youth to put their hands on either side, to feel it expand. As blowing commenced, the therapist engaged the youth, now in arm's reach and looking at the therapist, with some focused eye contact. Once moderately expanded, the therapist held the balloon upright, saying, "See if you can catch it," and let it fly around the room. The youth laughed, ran for it, missed, and the therapist said, "Try it again." The activity of feeling it expanded and then flying it around the room was repeated. The balloon was eventually tied off, and the therapist immediately started hitting it toward the youth. Once the youth hit it back, a passing staff person was drawn into the game, creating a group of three hitting the balloon in turn. Once this was operating smoothly, another youth was drawn into the game, creating social interaction between the two youth.

- Bubbles were blown over the head of a youth who was repetitively spinning a toy. The unusual sight of bubbles prompted interest and brief eye contact, at which point the therapist demonstrated popping bubbles with a finger. The youth tentatively popped a bubble, and based on the enthused encouragement of the therapist, started popping more bubbles and even attempted blowing some too (the therapist held the wand and bubble container). After a few trials, the therapist suggested that the youth "clap the bubbles" and then "poke the bubbles," and then the therapist caught a bubble and said, "Hold still so I can pop a bubble on your shoulder," followed by, "I will pop one on your ear so you can hear a bubble." Most of the youth were highly intrigued, became very focused, and were receptive to engagement in joint attention with the therapist on bubbles and different methods of popping, seeing, or hearing bubbles.

- Therapy putty was squished into the hand of a youth, who squeezed tightly with help from the therapist. They looked at the hand print in the dough, and then the therapist modeled making a ball out of the dough. Once they had made a ball, they rolled it back to each other, and after a reasonable amount of time had passed, they drew another youth into the activity, promoting reciprocal play.

- A feather was blown into the air by the therapist and caught, or if possible, kept aloft by repeated puffs of air. Once the youth noticed the therapist's odd new behavior, the therapist directed a puff of air to the youth, who may or may not catch the feather. Either way, the therapist would touch the youth's hand with the feather, saying, "Notice how soft it feels." Some youth liked the feeling immediately, while others were hesitant. The therapist helped the youth by holding their hand to keep it steady so that they could blow the feather into the open palm. After giving the youth a second or two to examine the feather, the therapist prompted the youth to blow it back, putting out open cupped hands. It could take a trial or two for the youth to get the blowing coordination down, but it became a game of reciprocal blowing-and-catch for most. If blowing coordination was unachievable, it was shifted to lightly brushing an arm, hand, or cheek, and then having the youth reciprocate to the therapist. Staff and counselors were drawn into the interaction to create a round-robin experience for the youth.

Fun, surprising, and silly activities promote rapid shifts in the sense of social and emotional engagement in the residential unit. Emotional engagement is experienced in activities that promote social interest, cooperation in a game, shared laughter and fun, reciprocity, and attunement to the actions of another person. These activities enable joint attention to an item and action sequence, which require that two or more humans work together, taking turns or accomplishing a goal in tandem (such as blowing a bubble to the ceiling together). Surprise or oddness is often the first catch for attention, which is immediately capitalized on by drawing the youth into participation. Engaging multiple senses keeps the social event fresh, maintaining the interest value for the youth, promoting repeated moments of eye contact, following directions, and striving for collaboration.

Theraplay benefits of social and emotional capacities

The therapy team use an intentional and focused emotional engagement plan in residential units, in classrooms, and with families. A team who had previously failed in the objective of broadening the social experiences of the child or expanding their recreational repertoire becomes successful in helping children experience social engagement using early developmental play principles in Theraplay. Benefits are observed and techniques are developed in each setting. A change in atmosphere and energy in a unit is almost immediately apparent on the arrival of a therapist actively applying Theraplay. Children are immediately intrigued, and even those who focus on their specific, repetitive interests could be engaged for short periods. Activation to interest, humor, or joy is typically the first effect when engaging children in these sensory and social Theraplay activities, which create positive energy for most individuals. Second, increased awareness of surroundings and the social environment is raised, creating openness to interacting with others. Increased awareness is capitalized on by drawing the child into interactions with other therapeutic staff or with other children. Third, therapeutic staff or counselors can quickly learn new activities for socially engaging their child without a lengthy training session. Rapport is promoted between staff or counselors and children experiencing each other in new and fun ways.

Various Theraplay engagement styles

Theraplay sessions on our residential unit are conducted in two different styles, depending on the needs of the child and the therapeutic staff. Style one is a semi-random appearance of the therapists throughout the week. The advantage of this is that it avoids the child (and perhaps therapeutic staff) falling into a strict routine that fun, social engagement times can only happen at certain times of the day. Children on the autism spectrum are prone to strict adherence to routines and lack of generalization of social skills or recreational skills to other situations, times, people, or settings. Randomizing the use of the Theraplay activity times promotes a sense that social reciprocity games (activities) may occur at any time and in any place (e.g., playground, sensory room, lounge, gymnasium). In addition, involving multiple children and therapeutic support staff promotes engagement with a wider variety of people, making it more likely that children will learn to interact better with each other, and might generalize these skills to family.

The second style is a micro-session with Theraplay engagement sessions conducted in the context of smaller or larger groups at scheduled times. For example, if a therapeutic team member knows that Theraplay is scheduled at a set time each week, they rely on having someone bring a clear agenda to a session with the child to promote their small group learning some new skills. In such sessions, it works well to find a small and contained setting (e.g., bedroom) for three or four children, therapeutic counseling staff, and the Theraplay therapist to build rapport among group members while working on new recreational and social skills.

At the end of either type of session, whether a semi-random pop-up event or a scheduled group session, therapeutic counselors or staff will be given some materials to use for the rest of the week. The materials may be a small bottle of bubbles, stickers, balloons, bouncy balls, clapper toys, or temporary tattoos. An instruction card may also be included as a reminder of the activities that could be done with each type of material.

Micro-sessions have become popular among some clinicians. A traditional session of 50 to 60 minutes, typical in private practice, is frequently unrealistic for children on the autism spectrum or with other developmental delays. Even a 45-minite session may push the limits of a young person's concentration and tolerance for social interaction. A 30-minute session (half session) is common among speech and occupational therapists, but some children will still require briefer moments, doing better if the therapist shortens the amount of time spent and cycles back to them multiple times. In addition, distractions of getting medication, using the restroom, or having altercations with other children may disrupt even 30 minutes on a unit. Thus, 15-minute sessions are more realistic, but some children start out unable to sustain this amount of time with continuous social interaction. For these various reasons, the micro-session concept is drawn up based on the idea that social interactions in everyone's daily life are often brief. However, many brief interactions still have a cumulative and significant social effect on a relationship.

The micro-session refers to moments of social engagement that last anywhere from 30 seconds to ten minutes, and typically around two to four minutes. Examples are helping a child put on a temporary tattoo that took 90 seconds; doing a rhythm with clapper toys or a xylophone for 20 minutes; and singing *The Ants Go Marching* while marching around the playground for three minutes. Each is followed by shifting attention to another youth or walking away, providing a short break from the intensive social attention. This approach is associated with increased positive rapport and a progressive increase in social stamina when doing social engagement activities.

Different approaches to Theraplay engagement times mimic the social engagement needs of a family setting. Certain therapeutic counseling staff are exceptionally skilled at using these social engagement methods and integrating them throughout the day, setting the stage for children to be more socially engaged by family members as well. Cheryl and MaryKate exemplified this approach, working together on a residential unit and as a team in the school. Cheryl would schedule specific times throughout the evening for specific types of play, including sensory play on swings, cognitive play with puzzles and coloring, and then social play using balloons, beach balls, dancing, and singing together. In the classroom, MaryKate would schedule academic work time interspersed with group social interaction time and short periods of class social engagement activities. Both had cultivated a sense of joyful fun that was interspersed throughout almost any activity of the day. Cheryl could often be seen leading her group of three or four on walks to the cafeteria or park while having everyone sing marching songs or popular children's songs together. MaryKate worked in playful games, songs, or ball play with learning communication skills, chores, and self-care. Any activity could become an opportunity for adventure, eye contact, fun, and a song, such as the *Clean Up* song, songs for tooth brushing, a spontaneous dance party, or a game of pushing the truck from person to person in a circle. This approach exemplifies the integration of social and emotional engagement into everyday life that we all hoped could eventually be transferred to caregiver–child relationships in the home.

Promoting emotional and social wellbeing at home

In the home setting, significant behavioral problems could result in a tremendous amount of emphasis being placed on behavioral management. Also, much additional emphasis is often placed on basic adaptive skill training for self-care, toileting, safety, and domestic skills. As task demands increase, behavioral problems might surge due to child frustration or inability to communicate needs, frustration, or other feelings. It is common for a surge in disruptive, aggressive, or self-injurious behavior to be met with increased behavioral management efforts. The unfortunate effect can be that a caregiver begins to feel as if their role deteriorates to a functional caretaker. As one parent stated, "I am the jailor of a very unhappy inmate, and we have no fun together." Reorientation to emotionally engaging and mutually gratifying or fun activities is the antidote for the behavioral manager experience. More importantly, attunement is vital to enhance a sense of connection and respond sensitively to the child's needs. Attunement refers to working things out with the other person in a pattern of acknowledging, empathizing, trying something different, communicating "yes" or "no," compromising, and trying again.

The following therapeutic and behavioral learning principles are practical for shifting the caregiver–child relationship to one that is more gratifying, promotes social wellbeing, and even assists with behavioral management success:

- *Marschak Interaction Method (MIM):* Use the MIM at the beginning of therapy to promote the concept of social engagement and mutual fun. While the MIM is an assessment tool, it is also a therapeutic tool. Include a couple of activities likely to promote fun between caregiver and child—based on observation of the child or clinical interview. Suggest to the caregivers that part of the assessment is to have some enjoyment with the child.

- *Feedback consultation:* During feedback consultation with the caregivers, highlight any moments in which they appeared to have strong social engagement or mutual fun with the child. Caregivers are used to being critiqued on their discipline skills, teaching skills, and behavioral management skills, so starting with an emphasis on emotional engagement and fun is a big shift in focus for many of them. Noticing specifics of what demonstrated the social engagement (such as eye contact, excitement in vocal tone, touch) is essential, as it increases their ability to be intentional about this in the future. Highlighting how the child demonstrated social interest and engagement (e.g., joint attention, eye contact, gentle touch) also helps make the caregiver more aware of the signs of engagement for future reference. Emphasizing what people are doing right is highly reinforcing and increases the likelihood that more of the preferred and therapeutic engagement behavior will be used in the future.

- *Video demonstration of Theraplay between the therapist and child:* Create demonstration video recordings as a therapist. When working with children on the autism spectrum, having a few therapist–child alone sessions is often advisable because it allows the therapist and child to develop a rapport outside the context of the caregiver relationship. Family dynamics have a powerful impact on the behavior of children on the autism spectrum, and if a caregiver is present from the first session, it can be hard to change the dynamic. By engaging with the child first, developing rapport, and knowing what the child does in a relationship independent of caregivers, the therapist will be better able to evaluate changes in behavior when integrating into the family. For instance, if a child uses good gestural communication or picture communication with the therapist, but in the presence of the caregiver engages in hitting and yelling, the therapist can feel more confident in the functional hypothesis that hitting and yelling are behaviors arising in the context of the child's communication to caregivers. The sessions with the child alone can be used to create video samples of positive engagement interactions with the child, which can be shared with the caregivers as a training tool.

- *Role-play and modeling:* Role-play and modeling are the best learning methods. Sessions with caregivers and other therapeutic support people (such as teaching staff, aides, therapeutic counseling staff, au pairs, and others) work best if social and emotional engagement skills are practiced before the session with the child. Practice activities together, discuss the intent, review what not to do, and discuss what to do if things go awry. In a session, model the activity for everyone and then involve everyone in the process. Avoid too much corrective feedback in the session unless something is being done that could trigger a serious problem.

- *In vivo practice:* In vivo practice is the optimal way to solidify skills. Behavioral science has shown that skill is best consolidated when used correctly in a real-life situation, but with receiving immediate corrective feedback for safety. It is why driving training requires road practice under supervision rather than virtual driving, lectures, or videos. Similarly, sessions with caregivers should progress from in-session modeling to the caregiver's increasing control over the session. Ideally, the caregiver does activities with the child in the home or community. Whether a child lived at home and had an in-home team come to the house, or the child lived in a residential school and had weekend home visits, the family therapy program made an effort to visit the home and guide social and emotional engagement activities in the home. If distance was a barrier, the team would assist the caregivers on community outings near the treatment center. In either case, therapy was taken outside the confines of the therapy room to enhance caregiver skills, maximizing the generalization of learned skills.

- *Non-contingent fun engagement:* Relationship building for most humans is built on mutually reinforcing social interactions. In other words, we interact with each other people because we like them. Children on the autism spectrum can be off-putting or downright socially avoidant. When behavior problems arise, the focus can deteriorate to a quid pro quo therapy (e.g., "If you do this behavior, I will give you this item"). In the realm of social engagement, we want to promote more generalized reciprocity and mutual enjoyment. Even if strict teaching, communication, or behavioral training programs are followed, caregivers must set aside times for fun interaction. The fun moments should not be based on having been "good," and not withdrawn for having "misbehaved." It is merely a moment for enjoying time together. Avoid worrying about the activity being developmentally appropriate, and do some activity the child will enjoy that will create social and emotional engagement between the two parties. These activities can range from singing songs together to playing "Simon says" to drumming to painting fingernails. Create a moment where the child attends, gives natural eye contact, laughs, and reciprocates some positive activity.

- *Attuning: noticing–commenting–acknowledging–reassuring technique:* Children on the autism spectrum are often poor at describing their feelings, but their feelings are often expressed in non-verbal ways. Part of emotional engagement is using non-verbal behavior as part of a child's communication and commenting on it. For instance, if you see a child pull back from a balloon blown up, you might notice it and say, "Oh, you pulled back. You might be afraid the balloon will pop and make a scary sound." The child nods, and you say, "I am only going to blow it up a little way; I want you to feel safe." The four elements of this kind of communication exist: noticing the reaction, commenting on the reaction, acknowledging the feeling that appeared, and reassuring by adjusting your own behavior. At the minimum, children find this regulating and reassuring. At best, they become more aware of their feelings and develop fluency in expressing them.

Conclusion

When a collaborative and trusting connection is developed between the child and caregiver, staff, or teacher through attuned engagement, attunement to emotional responses can be leveraged into an emotional vocabulary. Thus, the relationship itself becomes the positive reinforcer for many other activities. We will begin to see the child try new foods, try new skills, attempt academic work, or become emotionally more regulated. Engagement-based interventions help children create a trusting connection with their caregiver and a desire to participate in relational interaction, and ultimately blossom in their social and emotional capacities.

Chapter 9

Nurture-Based Interventions

The Theraplay nurture dimension has the most unidirectional action from the caregiver toward the child. This principle is very important for children who have experienced neglect or abuse and who have failed to develop trust in adult caregiving. Such children often become overly self-reliant at a young age, especially if they care for younger siblings. This "parentification" can result in insecurity in regard to basic needs that is just as traumatizing as actual abuse due to an embedded fear of never being adequate to meet life demands. In such cases, being cared for by an adult who expects nothing in return can be a powerful experience for building a sense of trust, social safety, and existential safety. It is also necessary in some situations to teach caregivers to give care from a place of authority, confidence, and strong boundaries. For example, adults who feel insecure or unloved may turn the tables on their children, expecting caregiving from the child to meet their own emotional needs. The nurture goal in such situations is to help the caregiver meet their emotional needs independently of the child, so they can establish healthier boundaries with their child and be the confident, safe, healthy caregiver their child needs. A combination of therapeutic support and developing natural, adult social support is part of helping the caregiver.

Theraplay believes nurturing care is essential to building a secure relationship between caregiver and child. Getting constant caring nurturance communicates a sense for the child that they are loveable. It communicates that the caregiver will take care of the child's needs, which helps the child internalize a feeling of self-worth. Regardless of an individual's age, nurture overall functions to build positive internal representations and regulate uneasy emotions.

A typical child develops caregiving or nurturing capacities when they are well cared for by attentive caregivers, teachers, and therapists. Vicarious learning through observations is supplemented by direct instruction from caregivers or other adults. For example, when very young, if the child has a scraped knee, the caregiver may hug and rock the child, wash the scrape, pat it dry, put on some antibiotic medicine, and place a stickable bandage on top. When the child is a bit older, the caregiver will give verbal explanations for all these steps as they are being done, saying things like, "We wash it to get the dirt out," and then, "We will carefully pat it dry, so it doesn't hurt your skin…see there, we do it gently." Instruction may follow for bandaging, saying, "Pull back these tabs on the bandage so it will stick on." The child may even be coached by helping a sibling or peer who is hurt. Thus, children are expected to have the social and adaptive skills to care for another person's injury or emotional pain at a relatively young age.

The care process for even a minor injury requires a range of relatively complex skills, which include: recognition that an injury has occurred, identifying the best response for the type of injury, acknowledging and empathizing verbally with the hurt in a manner that is supportive and not humiliating, providing physical comfort in the form of touch or rocking, and even using proper adaptive skills of cleaning, medicine, and bandaging. Joint attention to the problem and the relevant emotions is essential. If an injury was self-caused by falling from a bicycle, reassurance and confidence-building words may be relevant. If an injury was caused by a peer's push, acknowledging anger or peer motivations may be relevant to the recovery process. Thus, theory of mind and interpreting relationship dynamics is essential to developing successful nurturing capacities. Yet showing nurture and care to others is often hard for children on the autism spectrum. A weakness in this area may develop for multiple reasons, but much of this care is unilaterally directed toward the child. Particularly if the child has intellectual or cognitive limitations, there is an unspoken bias in the minds of the caregivers that the child is unable to perceive the needs of others or unable to learn to be a caregiver toward someone else.

Social elements include touch, tone of voice, words of reassurance, and seeking additional help. Practical skills include care of the injury, medicine, and application of the bandage. Children with either low cognitive skills or advanced intellectual ability may miss the social cues or lack understanding of how to replicate them. Many children with lower-functioning cognitive skills may not be explicitly taught to engage in practical skills due to an assumption that they would be incapable.

Of course, most nurture is not about an injury. Rather, it is about more nebulous social caring events, such as showing empathy when someone is sad, giving support when someone needs an extra pair of hands, or showing someone else that you love and appreciate them. A typical child learns social cues related to facial expression, body posture, and tone of voice very quickly, with limited formal instruction. As a result, it is easier for them to recognize the timing or need for responding appropriately. This implicit ability is cultivated through some explicit instruction and training. For instance, a father might say, "Your mother is stressed today; it would mean a lot if you gave her a hug," or "Your brother looks sad right now; how about you ask him what happened at football practice." This practice of reading social cues and instructing on how to respond is often supplemented by verbal discussions in which motivations and appropriate actions are clearly explained, and in which skills building is actively encouraged, expected, and scaffolded. In other words, a child receives an explanation of the problem (e.g., "We all need to share the cookies") and is expected to perform the actions to remedy the problem (e.g., "You count them out—put three on each plate"). Help is provided if the task is confusing or complex (e.g., the cookies are counted and handed to the child who distributes them). Children learn a lot through this model—explain, guide, and do it. Success is typically reinforced with words of praise, positive eye contact, touch, and a show of admiration and approval, ensuring that it becomes more firmly embedded in a child's repertoire of action. The integration of behavioral approaches to teaching and reinforcement integrated with the attachment approach of both promoting emotional connection and rewarding actions with emotional connection may be observed. The two are intertwined in everyday life. Skills cultivated include giving hugs, holding and feeding a baby, and giving words of love, praise, thanks, or encouragement, among many other related skills. Children and youth on any level of the autism spectrum will struggle with reading social cues. While many struggle with demonstrating the social nuances of care, children with cognitive limitations are at a greater disadvantage because they are rarely expected to demonstrate the full range of skills, or any skills for that matter.

We believe that care is strongly one-way, caregiver to child. We are aware that many children on the autism spectrum benefit from receiving unconditional nurture from caregivers in Theraplay sessions. At the same time, we should remember that the child on the autism spectrum does not develop caring capacities in the same way as a typically developing child. They need help to learn with explicit modeling and teaching to develop nurturing capacities. How, then? The Theraplay integrated behavioral system offers guidance on this quest.

Theraplay integrated behavioral system

Skills must also be modeled and taught in clear, repetitive, and structured ways, similar to reading, sorting, cleaning, or bathing. The good news is that the skills can be taught, which is one of the tasks of Theraplay and augmented by methods from behavior therapy. The nurture component of a Theraplay integrated behavioral system is about more than teaching the practical skills of nurture and care for others; it is also about helping a child feel a combined sense of safety, emotional warmth, and human connection.

There are four key sensory inputs through which an infant or young child experiences connection: physical touch (being held, stroked, hugged, kissed); gustatory food (especially food that contains fat and is sweet such as milk); rocking (being rocked back and forth has a soothing effect); and eye contact (attentive, smiling eyes). In addition, a lyrical tone of voice is typically paired with these experiences and becomes associated with affection, love, and safety.

When development is unusual in some way, alterations to the demonstration of care must be made or the child's emotional wellbeing is at risk. For instance, a child with food allergies that cause severe gastric pain may experience feeding as aversive. A change in food is necessary to prevent the association of food with harm. Many children on the autism spectrum have sensory sensitivities to touch, taste, texture, sound, and smells, which cause commonplace caregiving (e.g., tickles, certain foods, certain clothes) to feel aversive. If unaddressed, the child may associate the caregiver with discomfort and harm, engaging in socially avoidant or downright disruptive behavior. Anger to tantrum to rage reactions may express frustration and be used to actively push away from or avoid the undesired experiences. From a behavioral standpoint, this creates a shaping program of undesirable rejecting, social distancing behavior. A rage or tantrum reaction may work to avoid food, get carried away from an unpleasant sound, or avoid being held or dressed in a certain way. Once a behavior works to achieve relief or comfort or gain an objective, it has been reinforced and will be used more and more often. Behaviors that achieve success the most often are used the most often.

Steps for Theraplay integrated behavioral system

A healthy alternative to reinforcing unwanted behavior is approaching caregiving with highly sensitive responsiveness to attune to the child's signals. For example, when a child is crying—especially an infant—it most frequently means that a caregiver's behavioral signals of warmth, calmness, and comfort are needed. The description below is an example of sensitive responsiveness to non-verbal cues of a child's needs.

A primary counselor of a nine-year-old child said to the new Theraplay therapist, "You better take him to the bathroom." The therapist replied, "Why?" The counselor said, "He is going to pee, and if you don't go quickly, it won't be in the toilet!" The therapist took him, and sure enough, the boy needed to go. On the return, the therapist asked the counselor how he knew, to which he said, "I can just tell. It's something about the way he holds his body." Questioning others, they said the same about children with whom they worked closely. It might be tension in the body, subtle facial expressions, or a shift in energy level and play intensity. Some signals were easily explained, but some seemed to occur at a subtle, nearly intuitive level. Similar subtle signs were detected for hunger, pain, boredom, eloping from the building, and pulling fire alarms for fun. The counselors were observant and highly responsive to non-verbal signals. Furthermore, this behavioral acumen is positively reinforcing. Detailed awareness could mean the difference between a brief, successful trip to the bathroom versus a lengthy, smelly showering process accompanied by special laundry procedures.

Effective caregivers apply the same responsiveness to heading off challenging behavior to promoting connection and prosocial relationship interactions. Therefore, using behavior as communication—and responding—is central to Theraplay. The following steps are outlined in the Theraplay integrated behavioral system:

- *Step 1:* The therapist must learn what they can about the child's preferences, including what gives them enjoyment or comfort, and what is aversive. The behavioral approach uses a process called functional behavioral assessment (FBA), in which the therapist carefully observes the child engaging in activities across play, social interactions, school, self-care, and community trips. A good FBA will include a reinforcer assessment in which extensive information is obtained about what a child finds rewarding or pleasurable. Information is obtained from interviewing people who know the child well and through careful observation and experimental probes (e.g., testing out options). Theraplay also conducts a similar process through an intake interview, Marschak Interaction Method (MIM) observation, and experimental play sequences with the child. An integrated format is particularly powerful for covering all bases.

- *Step 2:* The therapist conducts Theraplay sessions with the child, trying out a range of activities and sensory experiences, remaining attentive to non-verbal signals in body language. The therapist responds to signals with acknowledgment and empathy, changing actions based on the child's behavioral communication. For instance, if a child shows aversion to the feel of a cotton ball, the therapist might say, "Oh, that doesn't feel too good to you, does it? Let's try a different object," at which point the therapist might do the activity with a piece of silk, a feather, or a paintbrush. The goal of this step is threefold: (1) increase awareness of the child's preferences and aversions; (2) increase awareness of the child's communication style; and (3) build trust with the child.

- *Step 3:* The therapist expands the child's experiences. First, the therapist will increase the range of sensory experiences the child can engage in with caregiving partners while feeling relaxed, safe, and emotionally and physically cared for. This approach may require offering new experiences and encouraging the child to try them a few times, despite hesitation or initial resistance. The therapist must find a way for the experience to be positive, reinforcing, and pleasant. Second, the therapist creates an expectation of responsive interplay between two people. At this stage, it is more than just giving up. If a child has learned to avoid hugs because something about them was uncomfortable, it may mean finding a way that a hug can be physically enjoyed (e.g., a side-to-side hug). Sometimes an alternative show of affection can be acceptable. For instance, children with low functional skills may find fist bumps or high fives more enjoyable and easier to tolerate than shaking someone's hand.

- *Step 4:* The therapist expands the circle of reciprocity skills. Children on the autism spectrum typically struggle with generalizing skills from one person or setting to another. At this step, reciprocity is explicitly encouraged in socially interactive Theraplay activities. For instance, if the therapist did a massage roller on the child's back, they could then hand the roller to the child to use it briefly on their back or the caregiver's back. Turn-taking is encouraged in games, such as gently touching someone's hand with a feather, hand feathering the next person to brush someone else, going around a family circle, or back and forth between partners if only two people are working together.

Reciprocity in developing nurture capacities for children on the autism spectrum

The issues for children on the autism spectrum are typically different from these scenarios. Obviously, children on the autism spectrum and their caregivers may struggle with the above issues and are not immune to trauma experiences. Trauma, safety, and insecurity issues must be considered and planned for by therapists working in the ASD field. Caregivers' emotional needs must be evaluated and addressed. However, autism is an equal opportunity condition, affecting all types of families and people of any socio-economic status. A high percentage of children on the autism spectrum are very well cared for by emotionally healthy, very responsible caregivers. The nature of the autism condition tends to direct children and families toward certain outcomes. The more extreme and dramatic the condition, the more powerfully children are directed toward the outcome. Children with a combination of severe autism and cognitive delay often find themselves well cared for but lack skills in the nuances accompanying social nurture.

Lack of nurturing capacities at a later age will be a serious concern. Thus, it is important that children have opportunities to develop nurturing capacities by adding the concept of reciprocity in nurture-based activities. Reciprocity happens in attuned interaction, which is emphasized in the engagement dimension. It can be translated into the skill of "serve and return."

 Zoey (see Chapter 4) was interested in hand clappers, partly because of the flapping motion they made. After the therapist and Zoey traded back and forth doing simple clap rhythms, the therapist had Zoey put out his hands by gently clapping the hand clappers into his hands a few times. Then the therapist handed them back over to him by gesturing for him to clap them on the therapist's hands. When he seemed confused by this new activity, the therapist gave hand-over-hand assistance until he got the idea. After that, he was able to take turns with the hand clappers, doing rhythms on different body parts, such as shoulders or back. The reciprocity was practiced in small increments over multiple trials, expanding his repertoire of ideas and allowing him to have a massage-type experience with them on his back. The activity was demonstrated to Zoey's mother to promote generalization outside of the therapy office, so they could practice at home.

Encouraging reciprocity in developing nurturing capacities will be a higher priority for children on the autism spectrum. Therapy needs to emphasize reciprocity skills to a high degree. Families will need to adjust expectations to allow and facilitate more social care for others during interactions, and children will need many structured opportunities to practice.

Chapter 10

Challenge-Based Interventions

The challenge dimension in Theraplay is associated with building a child's resilience and persistence in the face of difficult tasks or situations. Frustration tolerance is the component of challenge involving the ability to regulate emotions in the face of setbacks to accomplish a task, typically involving a delay in the gratification expected and recognition that additional effort will be required.

Relationships are embedded with challenges in multiple ways. First, caregivers provide infants with challenges in the excitement of seeing their child develop new skills, learn something new about the world, or overcome an obstacle. For example, a toy may be placed just out of reach, purely for the joy of watching the child crawl to it, reach for it, acquire it, and explore it (probably by tasting it). The caregiver probably expresses excitement through a tone of cheerful voice and warm eyes, commenting, "You did it!" By repeating these sequences involving learning to walk, climb stairs, handle a cup, and numerous other events, an infant learns to expect adults, and perhaps the environment, to present doable problems that will be interesting, fun, or exciting to overcome. This process is the beginning of developing an expectation for life.

Second, a caregiver provides tangible support and emotional encouragement to accomplish goals. Sometimes a challenge may be too difficult for the infant or toddler. The caregiver will then make the task slightly easier or provide physical assistance for the child to succeed. The child learns that the universe is ready to help with accomplishment through supportive relationships. Alternately, the caregiver may provide verbal encouragement to facilitate more effort, knowing that a little more output will result in success. The child learns to trust in caregiver judgment, believing that more effort will result in accomplishment.

Third, emotional regulation is facilitated and modeled in the accomplishment of tasks. When efforts to reach a goal meet with failure, frustration, or injury, the caregiver provides support in the form of touch, words of encouragement, and a soothing tone of voice. Strong emotions are settled, and then the child is encouraged to try again. Repetition of this process establishes a foundation for maintaining emotional calm in the face of complex tasks throughout life. As humans, we continue to require and depend on those same regulation cues (touch, encouragement, vocal tone) throughout our lives, representing a basis for the experience of empathy.

Lastly, the relationship is inevitably challenged as two people with different agendas and viewpoints attempt to collaborate and work together. The child may want interaction, but the caregiver may miss the cue. The child may want extra help, but the caregiver is too tired. The child is likely to express anger, and the caregiver hopefully responds with actions that repair the connection. This experience also establishes a pattern of relationship expectations across the lifespan.

The healthiest and most helpful relationships in our lives as children and adults go beyond functional-structured, fun, or soothing relationships; they are relationships with people who challenge us to grow. The most dynamic relationships are with people who support and facilitate growth. In this context, a challenge may occur in three formats:

- Collaboration: two humans work together as partners to achieve a common goal.

- Coaching: one individual acts as the guide for another, providing advice and cheering support to assist the other person in reaching a goal.

- Competition: two people compete as part of the goal of developing a skill and accomplishing greater things.

In the context of treatment for children on the autism spectrum, the ability to use adults as support for handling challenges can become distorted. The ability to handle emotions in a regulated manner may lack normal development. Clues that they are being supported may be missed due to poor social perception. The result can be lower tolerance for frustration, leading to tantrum behavior and aggression, lack of persistence in the face of failure, and absence of asking for help. Caregivers may become conditioned by disruptive outbursts to provide excessive assistance so that the child fails to develop skills. Limited capacity for verbal communication is a contributing factor for lower-functioning children and youth. Poor ability to perceive facial expressions or interpret social cues can be a limitation for higher-functioning children and youth.

Integrating elements of challenge for children on the autism spectrum

Both behavior therapists and Theraplay therapists have developed numerous methods for training resilience and improving frustration tolerance. Some of the skills overlap, but there are also distinct differences. A critical skill integrating elements of both approaches is to provide support but still have them do it, naming it as "doing with."

Replace "doing for" by "doing with"

One of the most difficult shifts for caregivers is to shift from "doing for" to "doing with." When a child is limited, it is usually much easier to do things for the child, such as dress them, prepare food for lunch, run laundry through the machine and fold it, wash the dishes, or any number of other daily tasks. Adults are much faster, more safety conscious, and more precise. It saves time to complete self-care and domestic jobs for the child, providing more time for other things, such as all the other chores that need to be done, or playing with the other children in the house.

Indeed, siblings will sometimes fall into the pattern of "doing for" their brother or sister because it means less hassle for Mom or Dad. Also, "doing for" may be part of the family culture, especially if compassion and cooperation are family values. Unfortunately, excessive "doing for" deprives the child of learning, and, over time, it diminishes their level of independence.

"Doing with" means taking the time to collaborate with the youth with limitations and find a way forward that includes active participation. Initially, this may mean arranging for active involvement in a repetitive action that is easy to do and is rewarded intrinsically or extrinsically. Pushing buttons to have an action take place is rewarding for many children, especially so for mechanically minded children on the autism spectrum. This makes it easy to start assisting with the laundry washer, drier, or dishwasher. Indeed, it can be part of task analysis for increasing skills (see Appendix 1). Machine operation steps can be modeled, and the youth is prompted to participate in each mechanical step.

In other situations, steps of a chore-type task can be made into a game-like format. For instance, caregivers could arrange a repetitive clothing shooting game when a child refuses to put dirty clothes in the hamper, saying, "It is a time to do a clothing shooting game. Let's see who is successful in throwing clothing into a hamper." While the child is always rewarded with a positive eye gaze, enthusiasm, and a high five, tiny candy bites (e.g., M&Ms) can be used as additional rewards to celebrate cooperation in putting all the clothes in the hamper.

This game is an integration of Theraplay and behavior therapy principles. Theraplay places emphasis on the power of play, social collaboration, and emotional connection as the child's reward. Behavior therapy emphasizes skill building, positive reinforcement schedules, and clear messaging. Behaviorally, some structured teaching is used to model and practice putting clothes away in a dresser. A specific reinforcement schedule is chosen to promote long-term participation. Specifically, a variable ratio of reinforcement is chosen because this promotes excitement and persistence at a task, diminishes satiation, and avoids becoming a "payment." In some situations, an M&M was chosen as the tangible reinforcer because it was small, highly valued, and resistant to satiation. The hazard was that the task could easily become mundane and lack social-emotional learning, so key Theraplay skills needed to be included.

Children learn through play and are generally engaged and reinforced by play and feelings of excitement. The Theraplay component of the approach is to emphasize the fun in what we are doing, make it a collaborative and cooperative enterprise (as opposed to a supervisory or teacher–student relationship), and send powerful social cues to activate attachment and social engagement systems of the brain. In the example of the clothing shooting game, the adult was clearly in charge as the orchestrator of the activity, but the enthusiasm and framing of the activity created a game-like feel for the child. Eye gaze with emotional warmth was used to promote emotional engagement with each directive and on each return from a clothing stash. Return was accompanied by naturalistic interaction, such as a smile, a high five, a comment on "how fast you were," and exciting warmth in tone of voice. These social-emotional clues promote social connection and a sense of enjoying the task for its own sake. Practice following directions was naturally embedded, so the child learned to trust that a directive given by a caregiver would be a good thing, would probably be doable, would be socially rewarded, and might be fun.

Inherent in the entire process of integrating Theraplay and behavioral principles is the unspoken message that the caregiver is a collaborator who would "do with" rather than "do for" the child. The message is "You are capable and can learn," accompanied by "I like working with you, and we will accomplish things together." Another inherent message is "Getting things done together will often be fun."

Of course, sometimes the task is not fun, such as cleaning tables or wiping bottoms. However, the principle of "doing with" instead of "doing for" remains. Often it is more time-consuming to "do with." However, if the child develops the task skill over repeated practice, eventually greater independence is achieved, and the workload is decreased for the adult. Admittedly, it takes upfront effort and commitment and requires a combination of structured techniques (e.g., task analysis and teaching from a prompt hierarchy) and creativity.

Challenges to opportunities

 Nate, a 12-year-old boy, had experienced abuse and neglect in his early years before being transferred to a new home with supportive parents. The adverse conditions of maladaptive caregiving had damaged his sense of self-worth. He was quick to experience shame in the face of even small failures, minor reprimands, or corrective feedback on work. Cognitive delays inhibited his success in school, while social deficits inhibited his success in peer relationships. Due to severe behavioral outbursts at home, during which he would damage property or be physically aggressive to family members, he was approved for residential therapy. In Theraplay sessions, the smallest setback, such as failing to catch a feather in a back-and-forth blow game, elicited a shame response.

In the classroom, Nate showed very low resilience in the face of frustration. His uneven cognitive profile made it easy to overestimate his skills. While some expressive language skills were nearly average, his abstract reasoning was quite delayed, and his processing speed was very slow. His relatively good verbal expression led everyone to assume that he could solve much more difficult problems than he was capable of, and even when a skill or concept was within his grasp, his slow processing speed led people to think he needed prompting. The combined effect of being challenged with problems or material too hard for him, or, alternately, being pressured and prompted to solve problems more quickly than his processing speed, infuriated Nate. Observing him in class, we saw him fluctuate between total shutdowns and moments of rage. He might give up on a math problem and put his head down on the desk and pretend to be asleep, or he could throw his books, scream, thrash, and hurl himself to the ground.

Learned helplessness is an extreme form of low confidence in the ability to effect change or accomplish tasks. Pressure to perform a task is met with low resilience or persistence in the face of failure, and a high likelihood of either a tantrum outburst involving crying, yelling, property destruction, or running from the room, or an emotional collapse response that includes social withdrawal and non-compliance. The responses from Theraplay therapists and behavior therapists have similar features, but may be executed somewhat differently.

Faced with adverse behavior patterns of tantrums or collapse in the face of difficulty, a Theraplay therapist will engage the child in a simple but fun task they can easily accomplish together, such as a three-legged walk across the room, hitting a balloon back and forth, or blowing a cotton ball from one person's hand to another's. The principle is to reduce the intensity or difficulty of the task demands while increasing the support needed for the child to be successful and feel a sense of accomplishment. Once some successes have been achieved together as collaborators, a challenge will be presented that involves coaching-type support, but the child is the primary actor. An example is a game of punching through a newspaper that the adult holds tight for the child. The task is presented as a challenge, but is actually quite easy. The reinforcement value of punching through the paper is relatively high for most children. The intrinsic fun (internal reinforcement) is the excitement and sense of power from smashing through the paper. Added social reinforcement comes in the form of therapist praise, excitement, and high fives. As a result, the child experiences increased confidence due to success across the therapeutic activities, and their resilience and persistence in the face of harder challenges increases.

In Nate's case, a combination of careful observations and cognitive testing clarified his problems. Once clarified, reducing the intensity of task demands and increasing positive reinforcements were implemented. While step-by-step systematic behavioral approaches were the main techniques to support him educationally, the Theraplay way of interaction was the ongoing way of scaffolding and strengthening Nate's internal state:

- *Reduce academic difficulty:* Instructions and explanations of all types were slowed down, and extra time was allowed for mental processing. In a team and parent meeting with Nate, the staff psychologist made this clear to everyone. An explanation of an upcoming event was provided to Nate, and when he seemed confused, the psychologist stopped everyone from trying to explain further. A full 90 seconds later, Nate laughed, said he understood and re-explained the situation accurately to everyone. He then made a mature decision on the topic based on his clear understanding. After this, the team and Nate's parents were more aware that Nate needed considerable extra time to process information. Easier math problems were presented with ones at or just barely pushing the edge of his mastery level. A mixture of easy and slightly challenging problems was presented, so Nate could experience high success.

- *Increase positive reinforcement:* Positive reinforcement levels were markedly increased by Nate earning tokens for task completion at a faster rate and having more opportunities for cashing in his tokens for rewards throughout the day. Nate enjoyed earning special treats, short breaks, games, or time to listen to music. Higher amounts of adult attention were provided in the form of checks on his progress, praise for his efforts, or encouraging words about his work. The ratio of intrinsically rewarding tasks to stressful tasks was increased as part of increasing overall reinforcement. After completing a stressful, less preferred math set, Nate was allowed to do the things that he enjoyed, such as cleaning a whiteboard or running a message to the office. Allowances were made for his slow processing speed, which meant explaining ideas, tasks, or daily plans in smaller increments than was done for other students. It also meant allowing Nate twice as long to process, understand, and respond. Team members would check Nate's comprehension by asking him to repeat what he had understood, re-explaining slowly when necessary. Extra time was allowed for some work to reduce the sensation of Nate feeling pressured. In other instances, less work would be given so Nate could finish at the same time as his classmates, receive reinforcement of praise, and have the gratification of finishing alongside his peers.

- *Incrementally increase the challenge:* New concepts and increased challenges were presented in very small increments with maximum teaching support. New math concepts were presented to Nate in small steps with lots of practice for mastery of the component parts. This created conditions of near-zero failure, an approach sometimes referred to as "errorless learning." Occasionally, a problem that looked big might be presented to develop Nate's stress tolerance and build his confidence. The problem would look complex, but was well within his skill set to accomplish. Support would be provided to get him started, and lots of excitement was provided when he completed it.

- *Motivate with interests:* Teaching to strengths also increased a sense of competence and pride and elicited natural reinforcement from the social environment. Nate gravitated toward vocational tasks that involved cleaning, delivering goods, and organizing materials. Aside from the sense of accomplishment, he found these tasks intrinsically reinforcing. They allowed him to interact with adults socially, caused him to feel like a meaningful part of a team, and he received praise from the people he helped. These intrinsic, social, and personal reinforcers motivated Nate to persist harder at vocational tasks than he usually did with academic tasks. He was motivated to overcome the frustration of new learning related to these tasks. His curriculum and schedule were increasingly oriented around skill building in these preferred vocational tasks.

- *Theraplay way of interactions:* Theraplay for Nate, the staff, and his family meshed well with the above. Providing short explanations accompanied by a visual demonstration was modeled. Easily accomplished, cooperative Theraplay activities were presented first, slowly increasing the challenge level as he demonstrated confidence and enthusiasm. Multiple methods of social reinforcement were modeled, including warm eye contact, excited and encouraging vocal tone, and affirming body language. Attempts were made to increase Nate's parents' awareness of subtle signs of shame responses so that repair and modification of the approach could be made quickly.

The consistent application of this system of teaching and reinforcement greatly reduced the number of tantrums Nate had, and reduced the frequency of emotional collapse or shutdown episodes. Nate persisted more on educational tasks, showing gains in his academic skills. Integration with the school community was more satisfying for Nate, his parents, staff, and Nate's peers.

Chapter 11

Parental Stress and Autism

 Sitting across from Jonah's mother and father in a small therapy room on the residential campus, the therapist was struck by the worry in his mother's face and the sadness and tension from his father. After every possible in-home intervention and outpatient therapy, their child had been admitted to a residential program for reasons of safety and education. Services previously had included parent coaching, an autism support classroom, in-home behavioral specialist consultation, Applied Behavior Analysis (ABA), therapeutic support staff to apply behavioral support plans and reinforcement systems, and a mobile therapist's weekly visits. While some successes had occurred, the school had expressed the opinion that a more contained and specialized education was necessary, and the parents had realized that everyone's safety was at risk.

Dad said, "I just feel so guilty leaving him here. I feel like I am failing as a dad."

Holding back tears, Mom said, "I know, honey, but what about our other children who need us, too? It's not fair to them."

Dad's shoulders dropped, and a look of angst washed over his face as he said, "I know, but it just feels wrong to give up."

This moment of vulnerability and pain highlights the deep emotional struggle for caregivers caring for children with complicated developmental and social difficulties. As therapists, we quickly learn to share what we believe are practical interventions, only to find ourselves frustrated with a lack of caregiver follow-through, irritation, or arguments about why it wouldn't work. "We already tried that, and it didn't work" is a statement that seems to arise frequently. Even with proven specific therapeutic interventions or teaching methods, it can be hard to convince caregivers to implement them on home visits. Knowledge alone is inadequate. The barriers to success are rooted in emotional conditioning, expectations of failure, and patterns of family dynamics that have developed over an extended period. An approach that addresses these social-emotional conditions is necessary for success.

Jonah was highly active and agile, with no awareness of danger— at least none we could discern. At the age of 11, when taking him on a community walk, someone had to hold his hand nearly all the time, as he could dart off to explore something at a moment's notice. He was completely heedless of traffic. Never having been injured by a vehicle, he felt safe around moving vehicles, and it seemed inconceivable to him that a car would be harmful. Perhaps in his mind, it seemed that vehicles would stop automatically for running boys. However, the safety risk demanded that outings be carefully orchestrated for safety, including safety locks on cars or someone placed between Jonah and the door. Jonah's parents suffered high anxiety whenever they took him on home visits, with other concerns as well. For instance, he liked to climb and had been found on the roof of the house on one occasion.

Jonah would pace around the house with a high energy level and was willing to eat anything impulsively. Once, while his father was preparing a special meal, Jonah came through the kitchen, grabbed a large handful of raw bacon, and stuffed it into his mouth. His intense and unusual behaviors made it very hard to attend or host social events, resulting in the sense of social isolation. Most parents can rely on their children after age five or six to dress themselves, use the toilet independently, stay seated in a car, eat appropriate foods with regular social decorum, pick up their toys, and play for periods independently or with peers. None of this could be taken for granted with Jonah. It was necessary to carefully plan all basic life skills, adding time and effort to every hour of the day, every outing, and every activity. Tooth brushing required physical support and supervision each morning and night, field trips required scheduling for bathroom breaks and bringing extra clothes, and orchestrating cleaning up toys or meals required special teaching strategies to motivate Jonah.

Jonah's parents struggled with guilt over having their son in residential school. Still, they acknowledged it was a relief to know he was safe and that professionals were doing everything possible to help him learn skills for everyday life. They missed Jonah, but knew that the time he was away gave them the much-needed space and emotional energy to attend to their other children, whose lives could become eclipsed by their brother's needs. However, even the sense of relief in having respite could trigger guilt over the very sensation of feeling relieved. The problem was that Jonah's parents' guilt feelings kept them from applying suggested approaches at home. Thus, Jonah, who could be compliant with a strict protocol of daily support at the residential home, failed to present compliant behavior at home.

The social expectation and cultural norm are that caregivers need to care for their children at home, and it seems like a betrayal of their values to feel relief at having their child away. Unfortunately, this guilt seems to result in "sabotage" of the treatment program. The term "sabotage" is used with qualifiers because there is nothing intentional about the times caregivers fail to follow the program. However, their emotional struggles and beliefs still interfere, at times, with therapeutic success. For instance, out of guilt, caregivers might allow extra snacking on food reserved for special toilet use rewards, rendering the rewards ineffective for changing the child's bathroom behavior. They might fail to have the child follow the rules or do chores, resulting in less compliance in the future. Jonah's parents would often do daily tasks for Jonah that he could have done himself, thereby eroding his independence.

The protocol that produced success for children and youth with severe cognitive and functional limitations in a residential program or home program includes the following components. First, a clear and reliable schedule is typically reinforced by a picture schedule containing icons that can be removed once a task or event is completed. A mix of highly preferred play and less preferred learning or chores is clearly outlined and interspersed with each other, a more preferred activity usually following a non-preferred activity (the Premack principle). Second, the therapeutic counseling staff maintain strict rules and boundaries, being very clear and firm about what activities are allowed at what time, what behavior is acceptable, and what kind of social behavior is expected. Third, a clear plan for chores and learning new skills is maintained throughout the day, fostering independence. If a self-care or domestic skill is being learned, it is taught using the same procedure each time, giving support through a hierarchy of prompting methods. Fourth, positive reinforcement is provided on a regular basis in the form of praise, high fives, special treats to reward good effort, and fun activities at the conclusion of a hard learning task. Finally, a high level of therapist–child social engagement based on Theraplay principles is used to create an emotional connection that promotes a positive working collaboration.

In the home environment, caregivers often presented "sabotage" of the treatments in the following ways:

- Wanting to show love to their child, caregivers give copious amounts of chocolate treats. When therapists try to use chocolate bites or other treats as a motivation and reward for practicing a new skill, the child is longer interested in putting forth any effort to earn the treat, either running away, hiding, or even pushing the therapist away. Caregivers said, "See, I don't think this positive reinforcement program really works for my child."

- When the therapist tries to explain that certain special activities or treats should be maintained as a motivational reward for demonstrating positive behavior or completing a difficult chore, the caregiver might argue, "That sounds like conditional love to me. We don't do that in our family. We want our child to know he can have whatever he wants anytime, and that we love him."

- Therapists try to encourage a clear structure for the day, using a visual schedule and alternating some harder chores with more fun Theraplay-based engagement times. Caregivers might post the schedule but fail to follow it by saying, "My son just took off all the things he didn't like. We want him to develop a sense of choice, so we did all the things he wanted to do on the schedule." When asked how the rest of the day went, they often report, "Well, he finally refused to do anything but repeatedly watch a couple of animation video segments over and over. I just don't think he likes doing chores."

- Caregivers might tell the therapist, "On these weekend times, we feel he should just be able to have free time to do whatever he wants. He works hard at school all week and has a strict schedule. Everyone needs downtime, right?" Later, when the child is asked to leave his videos and get ready for a community walk with the family, he becomes physically aggressive, hitting his father. Caregivers might say, "He got to do everything he wanted. I just don't understand why he acted this way toward us. We wonder if the treatment program has really taught him not to hit or be aggressive. Maybe you need to go back to basics in this intervention."

- Sometimes a set of social engagement Theraplay activities might be tried on a single day for a brief period, but with a lack of reliable effort over time, no change would occur. The absence of increased social engagement or absence of learning and behavioral change would be blamed on the therapists, with statements of "This intervention just doesn't work," and "My son doesn't like this type of program. He got agitated and resistant, so I think it just isn't the right program for him."

Caregivers' stress

The therapists might leave the caregiver consultation sessions feeling very frustrated, struggling to understand why the family is unwilling to follow their training guidelines. There would be a tendency to blame the caregivers as "resistant." It could seem that the caregivers are "sabotaging" the therapeutic interventions. This phenomenon was well described by Mark Durand (2011) in his book on parent support. He identified some key factors leading to the breakdown of parent–therapist working relationships, and outlined why parents struggle to follow through with therapeutic programs. These reasons include emotional struggles, hopeless thoughts, and a lack of understanding. Feeling a failure as a parent or guilt at maybe having genetically caused your child to have autism are common emotion–thought reactions that interfere with therapeutic success. Parental stress in caring for children or youth with severe functional limitations can be very high, especially when the autism is complicated by cognitive delay and limited verbal skills. Reasons for the increased stress include worrying about the young person's safety, parental feelings of isolation, managing life skill tasks, learning that the child is unable to complete independently, and handling behavior problems.

Caregivers typically experience a complex array of fear, guilt, worry, and frustration, all accompanied by fatigue. After many therapies for their child and family, they might also feel a sense of hopelessness. In addition, catastrophizing thoughts about the future are common. This mix of complex thoughts and emotions compounds the essential stress of daily care for their child, and amplifies the very realistic fears about child safety. Stress levels and negative emotions interfere with therapy success in a number of ways, a few of which are listed below:

- Caregivers feel so overwhelmed that any therapeutic suggestion or behavioral recommendation feels like too much to handle.

- A sense of hopelessness depletes motivation to try or to persist in the therapeutic suggestions.

- Fatigue dictates that even when a caregiver believes a strategy might work, it seems like drawing on energy reserves they lack.

- Guilt feelings may lead caregivers to give in to a child's demands in an effort to "be nice" or "be loving," resulting in fostering excessive dependence or reinforcing tantrum behavior.

Caregiver support principles

When caregivers fail to show enthusiasm or follow through on treatment plans, therapists will tend to react with annoyance, criticism, and blame toward them. Of course, most therapists will avoid showing these feelings overtly to the caregivers, but feelings of frustration build up, and it is common for therapists to conclude the caregivers don't want help, are sabotaging the therapeutic treatments on purpose, or are incapable of change. The result can be treatment termination, therapist burnout, or subtle negative relationship patterns with the caregivers. To counteract this and to obtain levels of parental participation in treatments, we suggest the following:

- Rapport-building time with the caregiver that includes time to understand the caregiver's life experience.

- Expressing empathy for the caregiver's experience and radical acceptance of where they are in the moment.

- An approach of joining with the caregiver (rather than "telling to" the caregiver) and acceptance of the idea that the therapist must do a lot for the parent–child relationship in the beginning. The overall theme is "do for," "do with," "cheer for," and "fade out."

- Supporting a change in caregiver perspective, which can mean taking extra time to provide psycho-education about therapeutic principles and addressing concerns or hesitations caregivers may have. This may also include traditional psychotherapeutic discussions with caregivers that draw on basic person-centered and cognitive behavior therapy skills, such as empathic reflection, examining underlying thought distortions or false beliefs, anxiety management, setting small personal goals, and having a plan of positive reinforcement for improvement (for the adults).

- Respecting caregivers' levels of readiness for therapy involvement. For instance, although Theraplay therapists emphasize immediate caregiver participation in Theraplay, they need to work on helping caregivers regain motivation to be involved in therapy by being sensitive to the state of depleted or stressed emotions if caregivers are reluctant to join.

Caregiver support procedures

The following procedures and examples are based on an integration of Theraplay and behavioral principles that we found to be very effective for parental change and support.

1. Use the Marschak Interaction Method (MIM) as a therapeutic tool

Over a span of six decades, the MIM has evolved into a streamlined assessment and therapeutic tool for family therapy. Initially considered a treatment planning tool, it quickly became an instructional tool through the feedback process to caregivers. In recent years, it has been recognized as a therapeutic experience in its own right. Particularly for caregivers of children on the autism spectrum, the experience of having a positive connection time with their child can shift their perspective about their child, create a sense of hope, and cause a change in the caregiver–child dynamic. The following example highlights this use:

 Todd, a 14-year-old boy on the autism spectrum, had been in residential care for over a year due to a combination of behavior problems that made it impossible for him to live safely at home. Despite a considerable amount of in-home behavior therapy, he was frequently aggressive to his parents and siblings if he wasn't given what he wanted. Social deficits and language limitations interfered with his ability to understand safety principles, converse about his feelings, or appreciate that other people were distressed by his behavior. Isolating himself in his room, he would demand food. If pressured to leave his room, he could yell, hit, and throw himself on the floor. Pooping on the floor occurred regularly, as he seemed to want to avoid the hassle of walking to the bathroom. Occasionally, he had wandered from the house, necessitating calls to the police to find him.

Todd's parents and siblings were extremely stressed by the time he entered residential care, but the worst for them was the sense that they had failed in their relationship with their son and brother. The in-home program had been lopsided in emphasizing behavioral management, with little or no emphasis on emotional connection and parental self-care. In that context, any sense of joy in the relationship had been dissolved in an acid bath of rigidly delivering consequences for difficult behavior, reward schedules for cooperation, task analysis systems for teaching skills, and crisis management procedures for elopement and aggression. Fortunately, within the highly structured confines of the residential treatment program, Todd learned to communicate his needs, developed appropriate social behavior for participation in school and community activities, and complied with routines and daily instructions. However, his behavior toward family remembers remained non-compliant. When the family was asked to participate in family therapy, they were highly skeptical that it could help.

Asked to start with the MIM, the parents agreed, but predicted that their son would resist the activities, fight against the hair-combing activity, and might become aggressive. The MIM was conducted in a conference room without other toys or materials. A camera recorded the interactions so that the examiner could sit outside the room while still providing a presence for safety. Mother and son did tasks together alone, interacting with squeaky toys, drawing, and putting lotion on each other. Todd smiled and relaxed at the start as Mom rubbed his back. They enjoyed the squeaky toy ducks, and Todd pretended to have the duck kiss his hand, imitating his mother's use of the duck. Leaning into his mother, he intently watched her draw simple shapes on paper and tried to imitate her. They took turns making marks on paper, spending three minutes in cooperative, reciprocal interaction. This was followed by imitating hand-clap patterns, smiling, and laughing together.

Father and son had their duck go for a walk together, give each other a kiss, and jump together. Todd carefully imitated Dad with the duck, and again, when building block towers, staying focused and responsive. Dad was very surprised when Todd actually combed his own hair and then combed Dad's hair. When it was time for a snack, they took turns carefully putting potato chips into each other's mouths.

Both parents were present for a few activities. Todd was intrigued by funny hats, putting a wizard hat on his father and a blue bonnet on his mother, and then enjoyed wearing the cowboy hat they picked for him. Using sign language, he finally signaled, "All done."

Coming out of the room, the father was smiling effusively and said to the therapist, "That was the best therapy we have ever had!"

"Really?" replied the therapist, who was thinking, "How could it be good therapy—I wasn't even in there?"

"Yes," said the father, "We all had fun. I think it was because it was easy, structured activities we could all do together. It was the best time I have had with my son in two years!"

This final statement was a moment of insight for the therapist, who realized that what was important to the father was having a personal connection to his son, feeling mutual love for his son, and enjoying their relationship together. If the connection was there, then they could weather the other struggles.

The MIM by itself can cause social and emotional change. The MIM experience was a point of change for Todd's parents in our example. By having such a positive interactive experience with their son, they were able to see that some true change had occurred while in the therapeutic program. They shifted their perspective from viewing him as a dangerous, recalcitrant child to a son with whom they could have a relationship. The experience instilled hope for a better future with their son through learning techniques from the therapeutic staff. They showed a burst of enthusiasm for therapy that led to increased effort.

This is common with other caregivers as part of the Theraplay-based therapeutic process at the center, although it sometimes doesn't always turn out this way from the start. In many cases, the MIM is used earlier in the treatment process, or certain family dynamics still result in significant problems. In these situations, the therapist capitalizes on other aspects of the MIM process to promote rapport and caregiver change.

Instilling commitment to understanding the child through the MIM and associated functional behavioral assessment (FBA): A thorough assessment creates trust and credibility. The MIM sets conditions for gaining a wealth of information about family dynamics and child behavior. Additional interview and observation techniques generate a detailed picture of factors that trigger a child's behavior and motivate the behavior to be used. For instance, both Todd and Jonah used physical aggression as a means of communicating that they wanted something right away. They used running away or destructive behavior to avoid difficult task demands. Their parents became conditioned to back off and give way to avoid getting hurt. Any behavior can have many causative factors and maintain motivators. A deep understanding of these factors can lead to highly individualized interventions.

When caregivers see that a therapist or therapeutic team puts a high amount of effort into carefully studying their child and family, it generates greater confidence in the findings. All too often, therapists jump quickly into standard interventions and advice without full appreciation of the history, beliefs, and family dynamics. If something has failed in the past, it is essential to know why. If something has worked in the past, perhaps it can be increased or adapted for intervention again. If a caregiver feels heard and understood, they are more likely to believe that the solution the therapist generates has validity. Thus, a detailed assessment of dynamics and behavior is a critical step toward fostering confidence in the therapists and the solutions generated.

The MIM and functional behavioral assessment (FBA) feedback and consultation are used to promote change: Watching themselves on a video-recording (in a supportive atmosphere) can promote careful observation of child–adult interactions by caregivers. This promotes self-reflection on how their own actions interact with their child's to create an outcome. Carefully placed questions by the therapist can deepen this reflection and self-awareness. Questions may include, "What were you feeling when your child did that?" "I noticed you pulled away/moved in—what prompted that?" "What did you suspect your child was feeling at that moment?" "Did we just witness a sequence of interactions that happens at home?" In most sessions of this type, a caregiver will gain at least one self-insight into something they can change to improve the outcome with their child. Promoting self-discovery for things to change is a powerful therapy, coaching, or teaching for any student in any field of study. The insights we gain for ourselves are more strongly believed, and the action changes we discover for ourselves are more fully acted on and integrated.

When doing video feedback, the therapist should amplify positive actions by the caregivers. If someone has a skill that they could use more often, they should be shown how they are using the skill and why it is such a helpful action. This provides immediate positive reinforcement to the caregiver, boosting their self-confidence, fostering rapport, and intentionally increasing what is already working well. As humans, it is easier to do more of something we are already good at than to learn a whole new skill. If every therapy session with a client resulted in a client walking away with a strong intent to use their good skills more, this would be powerful therapy. Highlighting what is positive and encouraging more of this represents the low-hanging fruit of therapy.

Caregivers will ultimately need guidance and constructive feedback on some things. They will see some of their actions as beneficial when they are actually counterproductive. Considerable re-education is required to revise their thinking about the nature of love, parenting, and behavioral reinforcement of unwanted behavior. However, video-recorded segments can often highlight these situations, providing concrete discussion points for the therapist and caregiver. Instruction at this point is often well received by caregivers because they have rapport, trust, and increased self-confidence. In some situations, video-recorded examples of proper social engagement techniques (e.g., Theraplay), proper communication training techniques, or proper teaching methods set a clear alternative pathway they can focus on. It is often easier to change a habit when a less functional behavior can be replaced with a newer, more functional behavior that has been clearly demonstrated. This is based on the behavioral principle of reinforcing alternative responses.

Small changes should be emphasized. Clinicians who are experienced in therapy techniques forget how hard it was to acquire all their skills. When consulting, it is tempting to try to have caregivers correct everything at once. Clinicians may be tempted to provide large amounts of information. When engaging in behavior changes, less is more. If a caregiver leaves a session with only one or two things they will do differently and will diligently practice them during the week, this is much more likely to produce success than hearing ten different interventions, five theoretical points, and six things they must change. Most will be forgotten, and the caregiver will feel overwhelmed and do nothing. Initial video review and consultation sessions should promote small but significant changes, and then lead to treatment planning.

2. Development of a working relationship with the child

For children or youth on the autism spectrum, it is recommended to initially conduct therapy with the child alone (i.e., without the caregivers). There are a few reasons for this. First, establishing a relationship with children on the autism spectrum can be more difficult than for neurotypical children. The caregivers represent a confounding factor when the therapy session includes caregiver and child. The child has inevitably developed behavioral interaction patterns unique to their caregivers. Suppose the child resists communication, for instance. In that case, it could be that the child lacks communication or that the child avoids communication specifically with the caregiver because of the relationship dynamic. The same can be said of play, adaptive skills, participation in chores, and the like. Working with the child alone for some sessions, the therapist obtains a picture of the child's interaction and skill levels sans family dynamics. Second, when caregivers are integrated into the therapy session, a change in the child's behavior is much more obvious to the therapist. Suppose the child suddenly starts engaging in self-injury or non-compliance or over-dependence in the presence of the caregiver, but not with the therapist alone? In that case, the therapist can be more certain that caregiver–child dynamics are at play in the behavior. Third, sessions with the child alone allow the therapist to develop a rapport and relationship dynamic with the child independent of other people. Rapport and trust are essential to the long-term success of therapy. If a strong rapport and sense of connection and trust in the therapist's routine can be established, this can be powerful leverage for making sessions with the caregivers more successful. The child will be more willing to cooperate with the therapist's activities in the presence of caregivers, perhaps overriding issues of family dynamics. The therapist will be asking the child to make changes, and trust in the therapist helps the child to make a change.

The therapist should know that their intervention actually works before teaching it to others. A therapeutic intervention that fails, or, worse, results in aggression or anger, can damage parental confidence in the therapy process. While it is impossible to avoid all adverse reactions, it pays huge dividends for the therapist to prove to themself and colleagues that an intervention works. When an intervention has been demonstrated to have clear success in a specific situation, if it fails to work in another situation, the question becomes, "What is different?" The therapist knows that the technique is effective, but the issue is figuring out what has changed in the setting or relational dynamics.

When the therapist knows that the child can enjoy basic socially interactive play, or even a small amount of imaginary play, this can be demonstrated to the caregivers. When the caregivers see evidence of success, the likelihood of parental effort goes up, and success when doing these activities with their child is increased.

Social and emotional interaction activities with Theraplay use a variety of materials, some of which could cause negative sensory reactions (such as lotion or cotton balls). Some may be too hard for a child (e.g., the mouth coordination required for blowing bubbles). Some children may have a very short tolerance for certain social games but engage in others for much longer. Certain activities just need to be learned (e.g., a song with hand motions), while others require practice in frustration tolerance (e.g., "Simon says," "Mother may I?"). The therapist should test out activities with the child, working out problems with them or eliminating them from the repertoire, if necessary. They should practice songs, games, and social reciprocity exchanges with the child until they are competent with them. If this process is followed, success with the caregivers will be very high, parental confidence will grow, and credibility in the therapy will be enhanced.

The same can be said for behavior therapy interventions. If a therapist thinks a social intervention will work, this should be definitively proven before passing it on to caregivers. For instance, one child with whom we worked was noted to repeatedly throw himself on the ground and vigorously bang his head on the floor. It seemed to occur frequently when watching TV. Seizures were ruled out, and psychotropic medication had no effect. Through careful study of controlled situations, it was demonstrated that task demands and sensory factors were not to blame, but it did appear that the situation was socially mediated. In other words, the child learned that he could obtain social interaction through injurious behavior. In this case, through carefully managed trials, it was demonstrated that giving some type of appropriate social interaction every 7–10 minutes easily eliminated the behavior. Once this was established and demonstrated, caregivers and other service professionals were willing to rigorously follow a program of social support on the recommended timeline. Socially reinforcing connection moments needed to be a prescribed part of treatment.

3. Collaborative caregiver–therapist relationship building

The therapist should develop rapport with the caregivers to provide the groundwork for emotional and cognitive change in their perspective. The following principle will hold a therapist in good stead: empathy before reflection, trust before challenge, and understanding before change.

Empathy is much more than just feeling for or with a client. Many therapists who feel deeply for clients may nevertheless receive low marks on empathy from them (Burns n.d.). Empathy must be tangibly expressed to the other person in a way that comes across effectively to them. Caregivers of children on the autism spectrum are typically coming to therapy with many painful emotions, ranging from fear to guilt to sadness to loneliness to anger. They may feel like failures despite having tried many things. Having their story heard and feelings acknowledged and understood is the crucial first step toward caregivers experiencing a sense of rapport and trust in the therapist. Among many excellent training resources that have been developed for improving empathy skills (Burns n.d.; Hughes 2011), here are some select examples of techniques:

- *Generalized empathy statements:* "That must be so hard" or "I am so sorry you had to endure that."

- *Restatement empathy:* Restate what the client said along with their feeling about it, such as, "So you tried using raisins as a motivator, and it didn't help, and now you feel discouraged. Is that right?"

- *Imagining the feeling:* "I imagine that if you have tried that many times and nothing worked, you might be feeling hopeless about change. Is that right?"

- *Imagining the thought:* "I imagine that if your child is unable to speak, you might be thinking it will never be possible to have a conversation with her. Is that accurate?"

- *Expressing affect in tone of voice:* If the client said with excitement, "I got a job promotion!" the therapist might then say with similar excitement, "Oh my! Wow!"

Notice that in three empathy approaches, the therapist asks if they got it right. Even if they got it right, they might still ask, "Are there any other feelings you are having about that?" It is common for multiple emotional responses to be elicited. Once it is clear that the therapist is on target about the emotional reaction, questions that deepen the person's reflection may be used (Hughes 2011). Standard questions include the following somewhat journalistic queries:

- "When was the first time you thought/felt that?"

- "What is the impact on other family members when that happens?"

- "Where do you go with those feelings?"

- "Which actions make it better/worse?"

- "What seems to help, if anything?"

- "How do you foresee things playing out in the future?"

Notice that "Why?" questions are absent. "Why?" questions can often come across as accusatory. Furthermore, if a person knew the answer to "Why?" they would not be sitting in a therapist's office trying to get help and insight. There is certainly a place for "Why?" questions, and they may be used judiciously, but the other questions tend to be accepted as non-accusatory and having interest value to most individuals, children included. An almost infinite number of variations on the questions are possible, and caregivers tend to appreciate the opportunity to reflect more deeply on cause–effect relationships, their needs and reactions, and on what has worked or failed in the past. Sometimes a line of questioning alone produces insight that leads to behavioral change. At a minimum, rapport is typically solidified through the caregiver sensing the therapist's genuine concern and interest, and willingness to deepen their own understanding. This level of rapport leads to trust.

Trust that the therapist has a positive intent, has all the available facts, and has thoroughly analyzed the needs is a key step toward a caregiver accepting training or new ideas that will challenge their skill level or fortitude. Obviously, it is also assumed that the therapist can demonstrate a level of professional expertise and training. Belief in the therapist's expertise is combined with belief in the therapist's positive intent for the family when a thorough assessment is combined with a depth of empathy and guided reflection. This becomes a basis for adequate trust in the ideas of the therapist or team. New ideas about behavior change, parenting style, and skills learning will challenge the worldview of the caregivers. Once new ideas are accepted for trial, changing caregiving behavior will be a serious challenge, and this will require a high amount of support from the therapeutic team.

Training a caregiver in new strategies that will include Theraplay, adaptive skill teaching techniques, and behavior therapy methods typically starts with increasing a caregiver's understanding of both the situation and the techniques to be used. Video-recorded clips of therapy sessions may be used to demonstrate how a behavioral strategy or social game looks in real time. Recorded clips may be used to demonstrate the connection between an antecedent trigger and the ensuing behavior (or lack of response). In either case—a situation of demonstrated success or a situation of concern—the caregiver is guided to appreciate the underlying principles at work. Once a caregiver understands a principle, they are much more willing to change by learning and practicing something new.

Positive reinforcement of the caregiver's changes comes in multiple forms but should be intentional on the part of the team. Adults need positive reinforcement just as much as children, sometimes more so since long-held habits require effort to shift. Positive reinforcement eventually comes from the children themselves. When a child becomes more independent, shows social reciprocity, communicates effectively, and avoids dangerous behavior, the caregiver feels pride, emotional warmth, connection, and relief, respectively, all of which internally reinforce their therapeutic parenting actions. However, these changes can be slow on the child's part. Thus, therapist praise, emotional excitement, and verbal encouragement are necessary to motivate a caregiver. Reinforcement in the form of tracking sheets showing skill progress, small tangible rewards like gift cards, and recognition of achievement (e.g., certificates and pictures posted on a bulletin board) motivates therapeutic coaches to improve more quickly and solidify skills more thoroughly than mere training and verbal feedback alone. It appears we all like our efforts and accomplishments recognized.

4. Parent training to build competent caregivers

No one has more commitment to a child than the caregiver. The caregiver knows the child the best, even if the techniques they currently use work poorly. They will take what they are taught and tweak it to make it work even better for their specific child. They will come up with solutions the therapist never considered. They mainly need hope, insight, and a clear path to walk. Thus, at the end of the assessment feedback consultation, the therapist and caregiver should discuss the treatment plan. The goal is not to solve all the problems right on the spot, but to gain commitment to working together and showing up for therapy. A caregiver may present concerns the therapist still lack answers to. This is where the therapist says, "We aren't going to solve all these concerns today, but if we follow a plan, I believe we will improve things. Are you willing to work with us?" The therapist promotes the idea that both therapist and caregiver are walking the road together, as partners in treatment. Therapists and caregivers can accept that change is hard, but hope is found in knowing people will walk the path together.

Parent training sessions are based on the applied behavioral principles of modeling, role-play, in vivo practice, corrective feedback, and shaping of better responses. Therapists will model techniques on video or in live demonstration sessions for the caregivers. This can include modeling social engagement techniques, assisting a child through frustrating challenges, showing nurture in a way that promotes emotional connection, and being structured and firm with good boundaries. It may also include modeling communication techniques, positive reinforcement of desired behaviors, when to ignore an annoying behavior, and how to teach a child using a prompting system.

Once modeling has occurred, it helps to have sessions for role-playing the different techniques. This is how therapists develop counseling skills, and how behavior therapists hone their behavioral therapy skills. Theraplay therapists role-play social engagement techniques in their training. It is the same process for caregivers. Role-play sessions with caregivers alone give room for open discussion that enhances their understanding of what they are doing well and why the therapist recommends a certain activity.

In vivo training occurs in sessions by including the caregivers in the activities. The most effective way to acquire skills, whether Theraplay techniques, behavioral management, communication, or adaptive skill teaching, is through practice under the tutoring and feedback of a more experienced person. This becomes the role of the therapist. Good guidance involves pointing out what caregivers are doing right and correcting ineffective techniques. Shaping is the ideal model. Success over time is achieved by helping a caregiver successively improve toward an ideal way of using a technique. As caregivers become more successful, the role of the therapist shifts to cheerleader, fading back from doing the therapy or just becoming a participant in activities led by the caregiver. Eventually, fading back more proceeds to termination. Ideally, natural support in the community is facilitated.

5. Self-care and self-reinforcement for caregivers

Caregivers will inevitably go through cycles of discouragement and stress, some stress caused by regular life events. Support in the community, such as respite, childcare, summer camps, and the like, may be part of the therapeutic discussion. Caregivers need time apart from a high-needs child to recharge their emotional and physical energies. They need time to work on meaningful partnerships with spouses and friends, and they need time to cultivate some of their own hobbies for personal development.

Some sessions may require traditional cognitive behavior therapy in which a caregiver can openly present a situation and how it made them feel, followed by an examination of their thoughts. Rational and irrational thoughts are accepted as normal, but work can be done to shift thinking to more adaptive styles of thought.

Chapter 12

Theraplay Activities Specific to Autism

The most common traits that children on the autism spectrum present are perhaps sensory integration issues, poor communication skills, poor regulation, and inappropriate social interaction. As repeatedly emphasized in previous chapters, Theraplay is effective because it focuses on helping children on the autism spectrum to be engaged in relationships and build skills in reciprocal interactions with the props that meet their sensory needs. In addition, having the caregivers in sessions helps enhance the quality of the caregiver–child relationship, and helps caregivers develop many skills to meet their child's needs better. We often emphasize that Theraplay activities are only used as vehicles to reach the underneath of children's needs, and it is more important to know "how we use activities" rather than "what activities we use" when working with children. Yet therapists also witness the tremendous benefits of Theraplay activities when treating children on the autism spectrum.

Theraplay activities fall into four dimensions—structure, engagement, nurture, and challenge. In fact, most Theraplay activities usually have more than one dimension. For instance, the bean bag drop activity that falls into the structure dimension can augment engagement with opportunities for eye gaze, attuned interaction, and shared joy, once it progresses smoothly. When applying Theraplay activities to children and youth on the autism spectrum, dimensions labeled on each activity may fail to serve its concepts. For instance, the bean bag drop activity serves as a challenge activity because it requires social sequencing, awareness of social cues, and joint attention, which are the greatest difficulties for children on the autism spectrum. Further, some props that facilitate sensory integration are important to add. Activities presented in this chapter are for increasing the social and emotional capacities of children and youth on the autism spectrum. We include adapted Theraplay activities and new activities specific to children on the autism spectrum, hoping to provide insight to Theraplay therapists on how to adapt certain activities to meet the needs of their clients and to introduce other therapists to a variety of Theraplay activities.

Structure

Enhanced structure is necessary in most therapy situations for children and youth on the autism spectrum. They feel more secure knowing what the activity is and how long it will take. Motor skills and social sequencing are hard for them, so they often need high demonstration levels and hand-over-hand support to participate effectively. Activities across all dimensions and therapeutic need areas will require enhanced levels of structure, including step-wise and errorless learning sequences, physical prompting, and clear but brief explanations. Since structure is inherent in all activities, only a few examples of very specific structure-oriented activities are presented here.

The subsequent descriptions are written for the benefit of therapists and caregivers who wish to use these activities therapeutically.

Adapted Theraplay activities

Balloon activities: The adult and child hit a balloon toward each other. It is common for a child with severe functional limitations to struggle with both the physical coordination and social reciprocity of this activity. Demonstration and physical support are often required, so it can help to have two adults (therapist and caregiver), one of whom assists the child. Have the child lie on the floor and keep the balloon in the air only with their feet to increase balance. Balloon walking is done by placing the balloon between the shoulders of the child and adult, and walking across the room while keeping the balloon between them.

Feeling a balloon expand: Get a balloon started by blowing into it. Gesture to the child to put their hands on either side of it as you continue blowing. The child is able to feel the balloon expand. There is a sensory and a social component. The child feels the balloon (sensory) and is connected to the other person blowing (social). Give eye contact across the top of the balloon. This type of eye gaze—brief, and with an object between participants—often seems less threatening, increasing the child's tolerance for some sustained moments of eye contact. Once expanded to a safe limit, count, "One...two...three," and allow the balloon to fly, usually to the delight of the child. Do this again, perhaps allowing the child to let the balloon fly on the second or third try. Finally, tie off the balloon for use in other activities.

Hand prints: Hand prints can be made with various materials. One method uses powder and dark cloth. Hold the child's hand and put powder on it. Then, with hand-over-hand support, help the child make a hand print on the dark cloth. If the cloth is large enough, the adult and child can take turns. Paint and a large piece of paper allow for making multiple hand prints of different and mixed colors such as fingerprints, finger smears, and just making finger paint designs. Some children particularly enjoy the squishing sensation and are intrinsically attracted to this artistic activity. Designs can be hung on the wall or given to a caregiver, thus making it socially relevant. A high degree of physical support is typically required. Washing off the paint with hand-over-hand support from the adult becomes a structured adaptive skill task involving water, soap, and a towel.

New activities with additional props

Body elevator: Tell the child that your body is going to be an elevator. When they are sitting down, say, "We are going up to the third floor. This position is on the first floor [gesture to lower the body by bending your knees and slouching your shoulders], second floor [move the body a bit higher], and third floor [full standing position]." Depending on the functional levels of the child, you can call out "Fifth-floor elevator" and even "Seventh-floor elevator." In the same way, call out that you are going down to the first floor when in a standing-up position.

Color play: This activity aims for attention, body coordination, and following directions. Before the activity, prepare pairs of six to eight circles of sticky paper, 4 inches long, and paste them onto the floor. Stand side by side with the child, holding hands at the start line, and say, "Let's do color play." First, call one color, such as "yellow." Quickly assist the child in moving on to the area with the colored circles and have the child put their feet on the yellow-colored circle. If the child understands the activity clearly, you can call out two colors, such as "red and yellow." For a child with adequate cognitive skills, take turns to call out the colors.

Mirror activities: A large wall mirror is an excellent prop to expand sensory activities and build a foundation for interactive play. One method uses lotion. Similar to the hand prints activity, hold the child's hand and put lotion on the child's hand. Then, with hand-over-hand support, help the child make hand prints on the mirror. If the child shows interest in rubbing their hands on the mirror, support them in smearing lotion all over the mirror or drawing shapes on it. Sometimes you may make comments such as "There is your gorgeous smile" or "Peek-a-boo" by looking at the child's eyes in the mirror, which can naturally entice the child to look at themselves in the mirror.

Another example is doing a movement activity in front of the mirror. Stand side by side with the child, facing the mirror. Another adult (or caregiver) stands behind the child to provide hand-over-hand support for a child with limited skills or understanding. Say, "Do just like me," making simple gestures such as putting a hand up, touching a nose, smiling, etc. If the child cannot copy the gesture, the caregiver (or another adult) behind the child can help them copy the gesture with hand-over-hand support, such as lotion hand printing on the mirror, smearing lotion, or playing "Peek-a-boo" by looking at the eyes of the child in the mirror. Also, add familiar rhythms to entice the child's attention.

Engagement

Engaging children on the autism spectrum often requires capitalizing on activities already familiar to them, including stereotyped actions they do repetitively for self-soothing or sensory enjoyment. Many engagement activities have components to help over-active children who actually have under-reactive vestibular systems. Since the major function of vestibular systems is to detect movement in the position of the head, over-active children tend to avoid body movements because sensory imbalance can be frightening. On the other hand, children with over-reactive vestibular systems constantly seek body movements to achieve a state of quietness. Thus, they tend to struggle with balance. Activities that increase balance, such as rocking activities, bubble wrap pop with lotion, or feet bicycle, will be helpful for children to improve their vestibular systems.

Adapted Theraplay activities

Annoying stickers: A traditional Theraplay game is to place matching stickers on the caregiver and child. A variation is to place a sticker on the child and then have the child put a sticker on the matching body part of the caregiver. The caregiver and child then touch stickers on the matching body parts (e.g., shoulder to shoulder, wrist to wrist, knee to knee). For children on the autism spectrum, this can be a good exercise in activating mirror neurons, helping the child increase awareness of how their own body parts mirror another person's body and actions. However, many children on the autism spectrum find the stickers disconcerting, disliking what seems to them to be an odd addition to their clothing. This reaction necessitates an adaptation of stickers, which nevertheless promotes a social exchange. A sticker is placed on the child, and if the child shows the desire to remove it immediately, the adult gestures to their own body part, guiding the child to place the sticker on the adult's body part. For many children, this turns into a good-natured game of sticker exchange.

Bubble wrap pop: Lay down a 3-foot strip of bubble wrap prior to the activity. Guide the child to pop the bubbles with their thumb, palm, fist, elbow, and feet. Then guide the child to walk, tiptoe, or stamp across the wrap.

Another method to increase sensory input and body coordination is to put lotion on the bubble wrap. Have the child stand at the edge of the bubble wrap while you stand on the other end. Then, lean to pull the child's hands toward you by saying, "One…two…three. Here you are coming." Give eye gaze across the bubble wrap. The child will quickly slide toward you, usually to the child's delight.

Feet bicycle: Sit facing each other. Then place the soles of your feet to each other's feet and attach them as if pedaling a bicycle. When you move your feet together, begin a song about riding a bicycle by changing the lyrics of *Row, Row, Row Your Boat* to *Ride, Ride, Ride Your Bike.* The lyrics follow as "Ride, ride, ride your bike, gently down the street, merrily, merrily, merrily, merrily, Sammy [name of the child] is the dream." For children with limited skills or understanding, have the child lie down on the floor. Hold the child's feet to sing *Ride, Ride, Ride Your Bike.* Once the child increases coordination, you can try the feet-to-feet bicycle activity to help the child experience rhythmic synchrony with body coordination.

Row, Row, Row Your Boat song with rocking: Sitting cross-legged facing each other, grasp hands with the child. Rocking back and forth together, sing the song *Row, Row, Row Your Boat.* This game is naturally attractive to many children on the autism spectrum who repeatedly rock as a method of self-calming or sensory stimulation. Rocking with another person brings this repetitive, stereotyped behavior into a social context with another person. Hint for success: grab each other's wrists or forearms instead of grasping hands for greater stability and connection. Clinically, this activity elicits intense moments of eye contact from some children. Do not require the child to sing along. Many cannot sing but will still enjoy the activity and engage in some eye contact.

For little ones, sit in a chair (or couch) with the child standing on your thighs, and hold on to their hands. When the child is standing comfortably, jiggle from side to side, singing *Row, Row, Row Your Boat.* This activity can happen on the stacked pillows when the child needs downregulation support. Place the child on the stacked pillows and then add one more pillow on top of the child to add pressure on the child's body. Gently press on the top pillow and rock side by side, singing *Row, Row, Row Your Boat.*

New activities with additional props

Flicking and flapping together: Many children on the autism spectrum will repetitively flick items such as string, paper, or blades of grass. This behavior appears to be a reinforcing sensory experience, but tends to be done with no social context. Flicking or flapping with the child can bring the activity into a relational context. The ideal method is to say, "My turn," take the item, and flick or flap it the same way as the child, up close to them, so it is clear you are imitating them. After a few seconds, return the item for them to flap. Do this repeatedly for brief trials back and forth. Clinically, this creates a rapport and relationship exchange.

Hand clappers: Hand clappers are plastic or wooden toys often used for parties or ball games. They have a stiff handle with a flat surface paddle at the end (often in the shape of a hand) and flat, hand-shaped pieces loosely attached to either side of the paddle. Shaking them back and forth creates a rhythmic clapping sound. Children are attracted to them for two reasons: the clapping sound and the flapping movement. First, show the child how to flap them, and then hand the clapper to the child. Some children require some hand-over-hand assistance to make them work, but they quickly catch on. Alternate back and forth between you clapping and the child clapping.

Hand clappers on hands: Using a hand clapper in each hand for maximum attention of the child, have the child put out both hands, palms up. Clap the hand clappers directly onto the child's palms for a short rhythm. Hand the clappers to the child and extend your hands, and gesture or verbally prompt the child to do the same thing on your hands. Hint: it may require hand-over-hand assistance with a single clapper the first time the child does the clapper on your hands. Once understanding is established, most children will imitate and engage in some reciprocity.

Light-up vibration sphere: Spheres mounted on top of a handle are produced for certain celebration events. They often have spinning lights inside and vibrate, activated by the push of a button. These are attractive to children with cognitive limitations due to the multisensory output. Show the child how to push the button and produce the effect, then hand it to them and help them activate it. Give a few seconds of experience, then say, "My turn," and retrieve it. Go back and forth a couple of times. Then increase the sensory input to the child by rubbing it against their arm or back as a vibrational massager. Hand it to the child and gesture for the child to do it on your arm, shoulder, or back, thus encouraging reciprocity.

Nurture

Children on the autism spectrum tend to have strong sensory preferences. Some are hypersensitive to certain stimuli or have sensory integration difficulties. Occupational therapy often involves repeated sensory stimulation to assist with sensory integration or desensitization. In the case of occupational therapy, the activity is often done to the child, such as sensory massage to calm the proprioceptive system, and as such has limited social context built into it. Children who can't sit still or are hyperactive need downregulation. Theraplay nurture activities can be utilized to calm down their sensory-seeking system, similar to occupational therapists, but engaging the children in such a way that social interaction is emphasized. Sensory experiences are intended to be nurturing, enjoyable, and cooperative.

Adapted Theraplay activities

Paint rollers: Obtain a tubular paint roller with the hand-held application device it fits on to. Allow the child to feel the fuzzy material on the roller, assisting them with running their hand along the fuzz if needed. Demonstrate the rolling motion and then roll it on the child's arm. Have the child take the roller and do it on your arm. Take turns back and forth, rolling it on the arm, back, or leg. Most children like this feeling of pressure and activation of touch receptors, and thus it serves as a positive, potentially relaxing, sensory activity from another person to the child. However, the exchange back and forth encourages reciprocity and awareness that other people might like the same things. Facilitating a theory of mind is important, and part of this is raising awareness for children that what they like or dislike may also be liked or disliked by others. Other sensory objects can be used in a similar manner, including small to large paint brushes, cotton balls, and feathers. This represents an adaptation from traditional nurture activities in Theraplay, in which it is only carried out by the adult toward the child. For a child on the autism spectrum, you may still have the child receiving more, but allowing them to reciprocate can be an important social awareness builder. When the child does the activity to the adult, the adult may comment, "Oh, thank you, that feels good," or alternatively, "Oh, that is too rough/ticklish; it doesn't feel so good."

New activities with additional props

Lap ride: Sit on the floor and place the child on your lap—the child needs to be small enough to fit in your lap. Then support the child with one hand and move forward into a sitting position (similar to a baby's butt scooting). Sing a song that the child likes to help them feel relaxed. For children who need proprioceptive input, hold the child's body tight while moving forward.

Play-dough or putty squish: Take some play-dough or putty-type material, and have the child press it into their palms. Spread it around with the child's fingers and then flatten it by pressing the child's hand with the putty between your hands. This gives touch and deep-pressure input that usually feels safe to a child. After a moment of squishing, pull the putty off the child's hand, placing it right next to their hand. Match the lines in the putty with lines in the hand. Looking together represents joint attention. Some children will be interested, and others will not. Either way, help the child do other things with the putty, such as rolling it into a ball or cylinder between your two hands, stretching it out in a long string, or just squeezing it very hard with your hands wrapped around the child. In all cases, proprioceptive and pressure sensory input is provided to the child, and the activity has become a social interaction.

Pin board sharing: A pin board is a rectangular plastic board with hundreds of metallic pins inserted next to each other that easily drop through the board. A second plastic piece prevents them from falling out.

When pressure from your hand or an object is placed across the pins, they create a metallic pin pattern of the hand or object. Many children like the feel of the pins on their hand or arm in addition to the visual pattern created. Many children also like the sound of the pins shifting through the holes or hitting against the plastic plate that prevents them from falling out. Joint attention can be facilitated with this by making hand designs with the child. You and the child both use your hands together to create a design. Another method is to put the child's hand on one side of the pins and yours on the other, and notice the feel of the pins as you gently push against the pins together. This increases the sense of pressure and fine-point sensation across each other's hands.

Vibration toy sharing: Toys that create vibration or muscle massage-type vibration technology can be used to engage the child and create behaviors of social communication and social reciprocity. Show the child how to turn the toy on or off, and then place the vibrating object against an arm or shoulder for a few seconds, careful to notice if there is a positive response. If the response is one of it being too ticklish or uncomfortable, it presents an opportunity to express verbal acknowledgment of the child's non-verbal signals. You may say, "Oh, that is too ticklish," or "That didn't feel good to you," followed by your supportive comment, "We don't have to do this if it is too ticklish. It's your choice." If the child shows a positive response, say, "You seem to enjoy that feeling," followed by, "Here, try it on my arm." Hand it to the child and have them try it on themselves, going back and forth between adult and child. You can also create a sequence of doing the sensory vibration on the child, who then does this on a caregiver.

Challenge

Children on the autism spectrum greatly struggle with many aspects of social dynamics, including social sequencing, reciprocity, awareness of social cues, and joint attention. Theraplay activities encourage these skills but generally represent a challenging growth edge for the child. Further, Theraplay challenge activities tend to engage children to stimulate their proprioceptive senses by, for example, hitting a balloon with a fly swatter, jumping off of pillows, or throwing and catching beanie animals, etc. The underlying objective is emotional connection and relationship with other people; thus, it is essential for activities to be delivered with high levels of enthusiasm and support, and with a step-wise process of learning that maximizes success and minimizes failure.

Adapted Theraplay activities

Beanie animal drop: Put a bean bag or beanie animal on your own head and then grasp the child's hands, lifting their face up to about your waist height. Say, "One...two...three," and then drop the beanie animal from your head into the child's outstretched palms, assisting them in catching it. Give an excited "Yes!" Next say, "Your turn," placing the beanie animal on the child's head and extending your hands outward, reading to catch. Quickly count, "One...two...three." Many children, even with low-functioning skills, will tilt their head to drop the beanie animal into an adult partner's hands. Do this back and forth a few times to encourage reciprocity and imitation.

Bean bag or beanie animal throw and catch: You and the child wrap around your waists a big square-type scarf to catch a bean bag or beanie animal. Each of you keeps three to five bean bags or beanie animals in the scarf. Guide the child to throw a bean bag or beanie animal and demonstrate how to catch it. Once the child understands the game, take turns throwing and catching bean bags or beanie animals. Do this back and forth a few times to make big body gestures of catching and throwing. For children with high skills, throw and catch can happen simultaneously.

Balloon kick under the blanket: Two adults build a tunnel with a blanket by holding it low. With the child lying on the floor, place a balloon in the middle of the blanket. When an adult says, "Go," the child can kick the moving balloon under the blanket. If preferred, the child can hit the balloon with their fist by sitting on the floor. Adults need to catch the balloon with excited voices to celebrate the child's successful hits or kicks. Use a transparent blanket or fabric balls if the child presents difficulty with noticing balloon movements on the top of the blanket.

Mirror game: This traditional Theraplay game involves an adult facing the child and slowly moving different limbs while the child, pretending to be the mirror, copies the movements exactly. This can be very difficult for some children on the autism spectrum. However, it encourages body awareness, and it involves the activation of mirror neurons. The introduction of the activity may require a demonstration with a partner prior to having the child do the activity. Some children benefit from an adult standing behind them, holding their hands and providing hand-over-hand guidance to participate.

Catch in a circle: Passing any object around a circle places a demand on the skill of social sequencing. Blowing a feather or cotton ball from person to person is a good way to start if the child can actually blow. Make it very simple and fail-proof by having hands right next to each other. Expand the concept to handing a beanie animal or other soft object from person to person. Once the social sequence is established, have everyone step back a bit and proceed to toss the soft object to the next person, going around the circle. If this skill is firmly established, social sequencing can be challenged by calling out "Reverse," at which point the object is tossed in the opposite direction.

Rock, paper, scissors, without rock: The traditional rock, paper, scissors game requires cognitive challenges for some children. At the same time, it is a common game that children need to learn to interact with peers. Show two parts (e.g., rock and paper) of three and say, "You can put rock or paper when I say go." Whenever the child wins, applaud them with praise. Once one set is clearly mastered, show the next two parts. (e.g., paper and scissors). For children with advanced skills, say, "We will do a new rock, paper, scissors game. When I say 'rock, paper, scissors, without rock,' you can only use paper and scissors to play the game, and the person who puts scissors wins. If I say 'rock, paper, scissors, without scissors,' we can only use rock and paper. So the person who shows paper will win." The tempo for this activity could determine the level of challenge for the child. This activity helps attention, impulse control, and cognitive process.

Walk–run–stop game: This game works on the skill of coordinating movement with another person, listening to commands, and increasing safety awareness. Hold the child's hand and say, "We are going to do a walk–run–stop game. Work with me." Then say, "Walk slow," and the two of you walk slowly. At some point, say, "Walk fast," and you then walk fast together; then yell, "Stop!" Abruptly stop. Other commands can be added, such as "Walk backward," "Jump up and down," etc. By holding the child's hand, there is connection and strong physical guidance in following the commands. Practicing stopping immediately on the "Stop!" command has saved some children's lives. It can be expanded to have multiple children and adults doing it together, creating a sensation of group participation and awareness of group cohesion. The activity is similar to the traditional game of three-legged walk, but is simpler for children who might be confused or unsafe with a leg tied to another person. It also facilitates awareness of coordinating body movement with another person while learning valuable safety commands. A three-legged walk could be attempted if the child functions well with this game and has good rapport with the adult leader.

Zoom-erk: Explain to a group of three or more that "We are going to pass a zoom. I will look you in the eye and say 'zoom,' after which you look the next person in the eye and say zoom.'" Immediately start by looking at the person next to yourself and say, "Zoom." Next, guide the child to do the same to the next person, and so on. While this sounds like a simple game that falls into the structure dimension for neurotypical children, it has some social complexity for children on the autism spectrum who struggle with social sequences.

On the other hand, it is simple enough that even very low-functioning children can learn to play. Once the zoom pass is firmly established in one direction, explain that it is time to reverse directions. For many children, this challenges them mentally to shift from a now-established habit and generalize their actions in a new direction. Some children are capable of including an "Erk." Explain that an "Erk is like a 'Reverse' card in Uno; it sends the zoom back the way it came." Demonstrate the principle with a partner and then try it at a slow pace with the child. This addition places huge demands on neural circuits for social sequencing and social cues, so be patient and be ready to terminate the game if it is too frustrating.

New activities with additional props

Ball bounce: Be ready with balls of various sizes and bounce, including tennis balls, foam balls, large rubber balls, and small high-bounce balls. If the child lacks good catching ability, start with sitting on the floor and rolling the ball back and forth, from you to the child and back. Progress to bouncing the ball back and forth, with small bounces. Advance upward to standing up and bouncing the ball back and forth. Games of catch inherently require sensitivity to social cues and turn-taking, and promote reciprocity. Interest is maintained by using different types of balls. The catch is a valuable life skill and developer of hand–eye coordination and cause–effect awareness. Humans of all ages enjoy catching, so once this skill is learned, it can be transferred to many different relationships and situations as a socially relevant and developmentally appropriate activity.

Flour dough activities: Prior to the activity, prepare flour dough (a mix of flour, water, and 1 tsp oil). First, loosely cover the flour dough with a clear wrap because many children on the autism spectrum dislike the sticky feelings of flour dough. Next, guide the child to poke with different fingers, smash with a fist, or grab with their hands to feel comfortable touching and playing with the dough, to have a positive sensory experience. When the child is ready, guide them to play with flour dough directly, without the clear wrap.

Another example is that you and the child sit side by side, facing a mirror. Doing an activity in front of a mirror is less threatening to interact and more fun to engage for some children on the autism spectrum. Take some flour dough and roll it into balls. If the child doesn't know how to make a ball, help them make a ball with the dough. Throw a dough ball toward the mirror and say, "I see your bright eyes right up there. I am going to throw it next to your eyes." Then have the child throw a dough ball at the mirror. Take turns throwing dough balls to support body movement and coordination.

Soccer in a circle: Soccer (or football) is an international sport, making any soccer activities socially relevant, developmentally and culturally appropriate, and mutually enjoyed by siblings, peers, and relatives, across most situations. Set up a soccer circle of three or more people. Explain that the practice activity is to kick the ball around the circle from person to person. Once kicking toward people is an established skill, introduce calling out a name before kicking toward someone. Encourage looking at the person to see if they are ready to receive.

Stacking cups: Cut four 3-foot-long pieces of string. Tie each piece to a rubber band to make four pieces of string attached to a rubber band. You and the child hold two strings each to move a plastic cup spread out on the floor. Next, stack cups to build a pyramid. The child should be able to hold two strings to participate in this activity. For a child with low functional skills, another adult can be teamed up with them to hold two strings together.

Toy car push: Take any toy car that rolls well. Sit on the floor opposite the child and push the car towards them and prompt the child to push the car back to you. Children on the autism spectrum will often have an interest in toy cars and trucks and enjoy seeing them move, creating an intrinsically rewarding activity for them to do with another person. Running a car back and forth is simple enough that children with very limited cognitive skills can still do it and enjoy it. It encourages social exchange and reciprocity, and transfers well to many settings with peers, siblings, and caregivers.

Chapter 13

Theraplay for Families and Children on the Autism Spectrum

CONNECTING AND REGULATING

Susan Bundy-Myrow

Introduction

Autism is complex, with many sides. Like a gem, it is most brilliant when all the facets can shine. So, too, in assisting children on the autism spectrum, we will consider the unique ways Theraplay flexibly supports growing children and their families in their journey to connect and regulate. The story of Jordy illustrates how Theraplay's holistic approach identifies and utilizes a child's core strengths, works through challenges, and addresses common concerns voiced by caregivers. The "I" here refers to me (Susan) as the therapist.

Jordy, Mom and Dad
Background
Jordy is a seven-year-old boy with sky-blue eyes that dart about curiously in search of details, his mind seeming agile and searching for something to say. "I bet he can do a one-man show," I thought to myself, observing his energy, verbal skill, and desire for an audience. Like other children

with autism who have advanced cognitive skills, he wanted to connect with others but did not know how.

Jordy's parents came in worried and frustrated because Jordy was becoming more irritable, rigid, moody, and avoidant of schoolwork. Mom became tearful while describing how his meltdowns were increasing at home, some directly involving his 12-month-old brother, Andrew. Jordy would scream, spin, and crash his body into furniture several times a week. On one occasion, Andrew was in his path and fell, but luckily, did not sustain serious injury. Mom feared she could neither control Jordy nor protect both children from being hurt.

Although quite bright, Jordy always seemed to experience the world differently with regard to touch and temperature, and preferred to have all of his items specifically arranged. He was a homebody, with Mom as his preferred playmate. He loved to tell adults about video game characters. In school, his teacher noted he was a bright, polite boy who stared off frequently. Increased involvement in the classroom was a therapeutic objective.

Pregnancy, labor, delivery, and Apgar scores[1] were normal, per maternal report. Jordy had been a surprise for the young couple, and Jordy's mother had reported feeling very anxious when he was a neonate. Family medical history was positive for asthma, learning problems, anxiety, obsessive-compulsive disorder (OCD), and paternal-side depression. Dad hoped to have a better relationship with his children than he had experienced in his childhood home. He remembered his parents as preoccupied and rarely playing with him.

Developmental history

Jordy's mother reported milestones within the normal range. Initial breastfeeding changed to bottle feeding given Jordy's frequent feeds and nighttime awakenings. After eight months, Jordy slept for longer periods, but Mom was still exhausted. At one year, Jordy was hospitalized for two days with croup, followed by multiple ear infections and asthma, for which

---

1   An Apgar score is a numerical rating of an infant's color, heart rate, reflexes, muscle tone, and respiration, which gives an indication of infant health.

he used a nebulizer several times a day. Although Jordy was described as clingy, there was no stranger danger with regard to the public, although he had always become overly excited and out of control when meeting new people.

Jordy's status included advanced vocabulary that Mom attributed to her early stimulation and teaching. Resisting new foods, his diet was restrictive. He was preoccupied with identifying and drawing video game characters. Mom noted that eye–hand coordination was difficult, evident in his struggle to neatly use a spoon, tie his shoes, and zip his coat. Frustration was displayed quickly, especially when time was limited, so Jordy's parents continued to assist him in dressing, brushing teeth, and bathing. Jordy had shown little interest in catching a ball and bike riding when Dad introduced these. Mom said that she hated to see her son so upset and struggling. She hoped to find alternatives to help her son.

Reflection: It had probably been overwhelming for Mom to be hyperalert for the next ear infection and to have to nebulize so often. It would be hard to be consistently present, to suspend worry, and at the same time calm a toddler who wanted to avoid intrusive equipment on his face. Would this process diminish opportunities to provide the affection, rhythmic voice, and caressing touch that regulates little ones? I wondered if I would see signs of both attentive concern and less attunement by Mom and possible withdrawal by Jordy. Allan Schore (2014) noted that as the infant on the autism spectrum orients less, parents may unwittingly assume a hyperstimulating style that may, in turn, increase infant withdrawal. The medical concerns could additionally have affected the dyadic interactions of the parent and infant on the autism spectrum. Both autism-specific testing and the dyadic attachment-based Marschak Interaction Method (MIM) were used to inform treatment.

Evaluation results: Evaluation results included average Wechsler Intelligence Scale for Children (WISC-R) scores, the Gilliam Asperger's Disorder Scale (GADS) with a score of 95, indicating strong likelihood of Autism Spectrum Disorder (ASD), and the Social Responsiveness Scale (SRS) (Constantino & Gruber 2007), with a T-score of 81, a severe range strongly related to a clinical diagnosis of ASD. Autism Level 1 symptoms included qualitative differences in *reciprocal social interactions* (e.g., trouble joining a group, happier when left alone, not responding when called), differences in *communication* (e.g., limited gestures and sustained odd play), and *restricted repetitive and stereotype patterns of behavior* (e.g., humming frequently, insistence on sameness, agitated when routine is disrupted, fixation on objects or topics, hand flapping, toe walking, spinning of self, and rhythmic or rocking behaviors).

The Marschak Interaction Method and SENC (Structure, Engagement, Nurture, Challenge) description

I entered the waiting room to see a sandy-haired boy hunched over a small table intently drawing something detailed. He leaped up with paper in hand and pushed his drawing into me. "Gold Pikachu is very valuable. I can draw Surfing Pikachu, too, and Shiny Charizard is old but the best one." "Wow!" I said, bending down, "You know a lot about Pokémon. Hi…I'm Dr. Sue, and you must be Jordy." Before he could launch into another lesson, I told him "The plan" and directed him to hold Mom's hand and follow me.

The video-taped assessments were conducted with Jordy and each parent over two sessions, with the dyad of parent and child sitting next to each other at a small table in view of the camera. Eight instruction cards selected from the MIM, set with corresponding envelopes containing relevant materials, were placed next to the parent, both for easy access and to indicate the parent's lead role. As discussed in the initial session with the parents, Mom had given an explanation to her son regarding their session (that I would help the family get along better, and feel less frustrated and angry so that they could have more fun together). Confidentiality was explained to Jordy, and the fact that their activities would be video-taped to help us make the best plan. He agreed.

For children on the autism spectrum, it is important to include MIM activities that maximize sensory experiences, such as lotion, trying on hats, squeaky animals, and feeding. Given their general strength in visual learning, the "Build one like mine" task is also useful. Singing a familiar song together can provide data on the caregiver–child's ability to be rhythmic and co-regulated with auditory input. For children with younger siblings, the caregiving of the dolly task can reflect attitudes toward siblings, cultural expectations regarding dolls, and models of nurturance the child has experienced.

The tasks for Mom and Jordy included the following: play with squeaky toys together; the adult tells the child about when they were a baby; the adult tells the child to draw a picture and the adult draws something too; the adult and child apply lotion to each other; the adult leaves the room for one minute without the child; the adult tells the child to care for a baby doll ("Do three things"); the adult and child play thumb wrestling; and the adult and child feed snacks to each other.

Mom maintained structure and authoritativeness. For instance, she read the first card as Jordy lifted her arm to squeeze under it to get a better view of it. "I can read it," he said. Mom responded, "I know, but I'm supposed to read it." She managed the organization and timing of the activities, and provided guidance when Jordy was uncertain. For instance, Jordy was hesitant to touch the lotion, but relaxed when Mom rubbed it on him first. "Aren't you going to put some on me, too?" Mom asked. Jordy complied using one lotion-covered finger and wiped it on her arm. A high-structured drawing activity seemed fun for them and extended for ten minutes in parallel fashion, until Mom asked if Jordy wanted to do a new task. In contrast, engagement in imaginative and reciprocal play was difficult for them both. When Mom asked Jordy what their squeaky animals should do, he was uncertain, and then appeared confused when Mom quickly moved on to the next task. Jordy rejected the baby doll play activity and said the doll looks like "scary red eyes" he had seen on a video.

Mixed results were present for sharing and receiving nurture. Mom seemed to connect with Jordy, smiling and gazing at him during a story about how cute he had been as a baby. When she told him about his croup and earaches, he touched his ear, showing awareness, but reached across her to read the next card and move on. Lack of preparing Jordy for change was observed when Mom only silently read a card that told her to leave the room for one minute. This change signaled Jordy to anxiously ask, "What does it say?" "I'll be back," was all she said as she left the room.

Jordy grabbed the card, read it, and started swinging his legs. He stood up and started to spin himself in a circle. When it came to feeding each other a food snack, Jordy was initially reluctant, saying he feared Mom would bite his finger, but eventually he accepted her reassurance and participated.

The MIM procedures were similar for the father–son session, but with a couple of alternative tasks eliciting the same Theraplay components of structure, engagement, nurture, and challenge. The tasks included the following: trying hats on each other; the adult tells the child about when they will be a grown-up; the adult tells the child to draw a circle, square, face, or something they like; the adult gives the child a piggyback ride; the adult leaves the room for one minute; the adult and child comb each other's hair; bean blow with straws; and the adult and child feed snacks to each other.

Structure was much less enforced by Dad and social-emotional engagement was less than with Mom. Regarding structure, Dad moved through the tasks in a perfunctory manner and missed cues that Jordy needed more support. Jordy tried to provide structure to his father, such as trying to instruct him to draw pictures for the drawing task. Jordy tried to engage Dad by talking about Pokémon, but Dad missed the cue. On the task "The adult tells the child about when they will be a grown-up," Dad briefly defined the term "grown-up" but did not apply it specifically to Jordy. Jordy gave signals of social-emotional engagement, yet his father lacked awareness or persistence in reinforcing these signals. For instance, Jordy liked putting a hat on Dad and receiving one in turn, but Dad ended it there. When it was time for the piggyback ride, Jordy said, "This is fun!" Dad helped Jordy jump onto his back and walked around the room with Jordy's feet dangling without support from Dad. Once around the room, Dad deposited Jordy in his chair, and then rubbed his neck where Jordy had clutched him.

Dad was more comfortable with functional tasks like combing Jordy's hair and feeding. Jordy enjoyed looking at Dad and combing his hair in return. Both enjoyed a bean blowing game, yet Jordy seemed ready to keep going when Dad moved on. After each feeding one M&M to the other,

Dad divided the remainder, which they ate separately, missing a potential moment of nurturing connection and engagement.

Analysis of the MIM led to treatment goals. The Theraplay goals for Mom, Dad, and Jordy are listed in Table 13.1. Jordy would benefit from increased engagement, structure, and nurture. Dad needed to increase structure, engagement, and nurture, especially use of touch. Mom needed to physically guide Jordy to facilitate regulation, and develop calming routines for herself and Jordy. She needed to nurture Jordy's successes and thereby increase his independent functioning. The general progression of treatment was to engage and structure or regulate while meeting Jordy's sensory needs. In addition, they both needed to practice taking the lead in sessions and at home.

An initial task in therapy was creating the neuroception of safety (Porges 2015, 2017). This was done via music, attuned touch and eye contact, and structured guidance. Theraplay activities were designed around proactive emotional regulation, modeling of structure, and building social interest and comprehension. Home issues were addressed via parent coaching sessions, "pack-n-port" strategies (activities that can be translated from therapy session to home care) (Bundy-Myrow 2000), increasing inter-parent support, and facilitating a unified view of their child. Visual materials, important for children on the autism spectrum, were incorporated into sessions as characteristics like Jordy's sky-blue eyes and strong muscles, preferences like cool mint-smelling lotion, and accomplishments like balancing on four pillows were discovered. Given his interest in drawing, at the end of each session Jordy would draw a picture of the "discovery of the day" while feedback was given to Mom. These pictures became the pages of his Theraplay book, "All about me, Jordy."

Table 13.1. Theraplay goals by dimension for Mom, Dad, and Jordy

Dimension	Mom	Dad	Jordy
Structure	Provide clear directions Model and physically guide Jordy for optimal regulation	Provide clear, positive directions Model and physically guide Jordy	Follow Mom and Dad's lead in activities

cont.

Dimension	Mom	Dad	Jordy
Engagement	Notice and acknowledge Jordy's feeling states and experiences Increase and maintain interactions Notice her own feelings	Notice Jordy's face Increase and maintain reciprocal interactions Initiate interactions with Jordy	With Dad, increase attention, participation, and enjoyment Enjoy interactions with Mom for longer time
Nurture	Adjust own behavior to comfort Jordy Help Jordy to use calming routines	Downregulate and calm Jordy, especially with touch Change expectation to allow more time and practice for Jordy and Dad to "grow together"	Increase assurance and acceptance of care Accept nurturing touch from Dad Practice self-soothing routines
Challenge	Encourage steps of mastery and independence Calm own anxiety regarding Jordy being distressed at times	Challenge Jordy to practice up- and downregulating interactions together	Manage the strength, force, and rate of physical interactions Practice "I can do this!"

Theoretical note: A Theraplay therapist working with children on the autism spectrum can identify the components that Theraplay shares with behavioral colleagues in the areas of social motivation and social communication (Bottema-Beutel *et al.* 2014; Koegel & Koegel 2018). Including a child's interest can be a point of "joining with" the child and a point from which that interest or preoccupation can be expanded (e.g., from isolated rocking to and fro to making a two-person rocking chair by holding hands, sitting feet to feet and making the rocking chair "go" by looking at each other). Engaging music and hand motions can be used for a full sensorimotor experience in a social context (e.g., *Row, Row, Row the Boat*). Theraplay uses sounds, melodies, and rhythms (think drums) to establish *shared* experiences that become socially motivating and guide the human interactions for children on the autism spectrum.

Theraplay treatment for Jordy and his parents
Parent coaching

During the MIM review, the parents could see how "young" Jordy seemed on the MIM and how he needed more reciprocity with each of them in different ways. I demonstrated activities I would do in Session 1 with Mom. She was eager to learn.

Session 1, Mom and Jordy

This boy was different from the chatty one I had met at the MIM. Jordy clung to his mother as if melting into her body. Building on this, I suggested they hold tight to each other while walking to the playroom in a "three-legged walk," to see if they could keep their inside legs stuck together! Mom knew what I was talking about and showed Jordy. We needed more structure and I threw a pillow on top of the bean bag, hoping it would help Jordy upregulate his body and arousal level. "Let's see how tall you are standing on top of this pillow and bean bag! I bet you're taller than Mom and me!" I instructed Mom to hold one hand and I took the other. "Okay, Mom, on three, Jordy's going to step high onto this pillow. One...two...three...whoosh!" And he was up, smiled a little, and held tight to Mom's shoulder. We marveled at how tall he was, and with our hands still together, I stretched our arms toward the ceiling. "Jordy, looks like you can almost touch the ceiling!" He smiled and stretched himself a little more. Acting as spotters on each side of him, I told Mom that we would help Jordy jump up and land sitting right on the pillow. He liked landing with a thump on the pillow and Mom sat proximally on another pillow.

Unlike some children, Jordy had not experienced one-to-one work with speech therapy, occupational therapy, etc. When he was in the presence of another adult, he would either cling to Mom's side and try to verbally respond, or hide behind her. "Let's see what else you brought with you besides strong legs. I bet you have big arm muscles, too!" and I pulled out a measuring tape. He smiled a little more when I told him I'd write how big each arm was and he could draw a picture if he liked. We were going to have a discovery every time. Jordy nervously looked away, and intermittently, to Mom. Mom wanted Jordy to be successful and directed and answered for him. As I introduced "Guess the goodies snack," Jordy wanted to give a snack to Mom. I said, "That's really nice to share, Jordy. Here's how we're going to do it. We'll make a circle," as I pointed my finger from Mom to Jordy and back to me. "I give to Mom, and she'll give to you. If there's a snack you don't like, you don't have to eat it. Mom told me some things you like, though!" Because of his hesitancy at being fed on the MIM, I showed him all the snack pieces in the envelope marked "Special." I said, "Okay, Mom, you both know all the snacks now. I'm going to hide one in my hand, give it to you to taste, and you tell me which one you think it is. Jordy, you watch Mom's face to see if she likes it!" When Jordy started to recite a list of things *he* liked, I held his hand and whispered, "Look at Mom's face! Do you think she likes the pretzel I gave her?" He nodded and then enjoyed his turn, telling Mom which one(s) he wanted. We held hands and sang a rhythmic good-bye song and Jordy eagerly drew a picture of his big muscles, standing on the pillow, and all the snacks he liked!

Therapeutic note: Whereas some parent–child dyads can start Theraplay together from the start, it became clear that I needed more time to develop Jordy's comfort level without Mom present. Simultaneously, I needed to strengthen Mom's ability to structure and feel confident expecting that her child could attend to her lead. Jordy's pattern of merging with his mother was so ingrained that we needed to teach and shape different behavior. In Theraplay, I call this the "three times rule." The first time is the child experiencing something different; the second time is the child's attempted return to the old familiar behavior; and the third time is tentative acceptance and comprehension.

Session 2, Jordy

Having explained the new plan to Mom, I entered the waiting room and welcomed Jordy right away to model the need for a greeting. I said, "Jordy and I are discovering some new things together, Mom. He can tell you all about it at the end!" Jordy followed me hesitantly, but brightened when I wondered how Pokémon characters would walk down the hall. We waddled down the hall like ducks, and "sticking together," he led me to the familiar pillow-topped bean bag. He looked hesitantly at the door as if wishing Mom would magically appear, but held tight to my hand and hoisted himself on to the pillow. I placed his hands on my shoulders, saying, "I wonder if you can squish the pillow when you jump." We started a synchronous proprioceptive pattern of jumping as I stood on the ground and helped him "jump–squish." With better eye contact and a calmer body now, Jordy said, "I can put this in my book!" "You tried another new thing and you did it," I said cheerily. "Let's discover some more!" As part of the check-in, Jordy and I continued to explore his comfort and preferences via a "sensory assessment." We checked his preference of lotion smells, his perception of temperature, and the kind of touch he liked via Theraplay games. I noted each discovery, and Jordy proudly told Mom at the end.

Session 3, Jordy

I started with Jordy, alone, and we made a "hiding surprise" for Mom to find him. Jordy loved to hide; this was one activity that he already cooperatively played with his little brother at home. The hiding reunion became a pivotal point in this session for Mom and Jordy's relationship. After the reunion and big hug from Mom, however, Jordy quickly went off task, verbally or physically enacting his familiar pattern. I needed to help Mom to physically guide him, to maintain his attention rather than letting him pull away. He would need to feel supported and understood so he could calm as well as re-engage when ready.

Session 4, parent update with parents alone

Jordy was enjoying Theraplay; next was to increase regulation. Video footage was reviewed and both Jordy's reactions and parental reactions were discussed. We noticed that Jordy was present-focused and relaxed during our opening and closing songs. Mom said she had enjoyed singing to her boy when he was a baby, and we developed a calming song that cued slow exhalations for use in sessions and home. To the tune of *Oh, My Darling*, Mom would soon teach Jordy: "Oh my Jordy, Oh my Jordy, Oh my Jordy, take your time! First your slow breaths, let your feet rest, hug yourself and count to five!" We decided Mom would participate and increasingly lead activities in our next three sessions.

Sessions 5, 6, 7, with Mom

I started the next session with a check-in and setting up a hiding surprise for Mom's entry. Jordy was excited when Mom came in and found him. But he began to spin and pull away. It was an opportune time to intervene and practice calming. I grasped Jordy's hand while saying, "Let's hold hands!" as we circled the pillows, counting down "Three...two...one... sit down." I sat behind Jordy to be his "safe chair" and Mom, practicing leading, sat knee-to-knee, facing him. Mom slowly rocked him side to side, singing *Oh, My Jordy!* He quieted and they hugged. I guided them to the next activity, wiggle in, wiggle out, in which "hugs," gross motor modulation, and Mom's structure would continue. Mom simultaneously looked stronger and more relaxed. Jordy's blue eyes glistened as he hugged her tightly and checked her eyes for the next "eye signal" to wiggle backwards to the start line. From that point on, Mom was present from the start of all subsequent sessions. She practiced maintaining structure, engagement, and calming nurture. Jordy practiced following "one more time" and waiting for the next direction.

Session 8, parents only

At home, Mom was incorporating *Oh, My Jordy!* before homework and bedtime routines. She looked forward to telling me that on one occasion, when Jordy had begun to move too fast and hard with his brother, he suddenly stopped and began a slow breath "when I simply started humming the song." She was feeling more confident at home, and the couple now felt Dad and Jordy could benefit together with Theraplay.

Sessions 9, 10, 11, with Dad

The first time Dad joined a session, Jordy dragged his feet and avoided looking at both Dad and me. "This is new to have Dad join us, isn't it?" I said, using his non-verbal behavior as his communication. He nodded and then told Dad where to sit! I remembered the two had had brief moments of enjoyment on the MIM, but it was not the norm. Dad followed my lead to focus on joining Jordy, piquing his curiosity and providing sensory input. Bean blow was a good choice because it was interactive, could be played as a team rather than win or lose, and it would culminate with a snack. When Dad told his son the rules of the game, Jordy threw his straw on the floor, moved away, and started to spin. Dad looked surprised and hurt at this avoidance. Grasping Jordy's hand, I circled with him and said, "Jordy, we need to take a breath in these pillows! Three...two...one... down!" I rubbed his back and invited Dad to sit closer. I said, "Something must have been really different about that bean game, Jordy, but I'm not sure what." Fighting back tears and mumbling in the pillow, I heard, "Dad didn't do it right." We acknowledged it was a new, different way, and that was hard for Jordy. We agreed to practice another time. We ended with a calming, interactive activity called "Drink and blink." Sitting knee-to-knee with pillows as his back rest, Jordy drank a beverage with a straw following Dad's playful directions (e.g., drink when Dad touches his nose and stop when Dad blinks his eyes). Jordy softened as Dad smiled at how well Jordy followed. As Jordy asked to make his drawing, Dad asked me why Jordy was "bossing him around." He said, "He does it at home and it's extremely annoying!" This was a great chance to be a "social translator." I explained that with autism it's hard to understand what's happening next and how it's supposed to go. "When he starts to boss you, it's a sign he's needing you to tell him *the plan*. He doesn't mean to be disrespectful. If things are predictable and 'the right way,' then all's well in Jordy's world." Dad seemed to accept this explanation.

We continued to focus on physical activities that engaged Jordy's curiosity and need for sensory input to explore play together. Jordy began to trust Dad and feel understood, and was able to tolerate faster games, such as Dad leading a "Red light/green light" game. Jordy made increased eye contact in magic carpet ride and bean blow. Cooperative game experiences like balancing a snack on a big pillow held between them and balloon balance led to Jordy wanting to play with Dad at home.

Session 12, parents meeting only

We discussed new routines Mom had begun practicing at home, and using *the relationship as a source of stress reduction* rather than screens (iPad and video games). Jordy had been having frequent temper tantrums when Mom told him it was time to stop screen time. She had begun practicing Theraplay activities learned in session with Jordy when he returned home from school during his baby brother's nap. Mom and Jordy enjoyed the close, playful time that included a welcoming check-in, a challenging engagement activity next, followed by a nurturing snack activity and their special handshake. Mom told me how she could feel Jordy relax as they sat on the rug together, his back facing her so she could "draw" the day's weather on his back. For instance, she might say, "We woke this morning and there were little clouds in the sky," as she drew puffy clouds on his back. "And then bright sun brought streams of light to the ground," she would continue, pressing more firmly and making a circle with lines that tickled Jordy. He would giggle and respond well to her firm squeeze. For challenge and eye contact, she practiced Theraplay's version of "Mother may I?" with the added challenge of Jordy balancing on top of two pillows as he followed Mom's directions. This required effort and concentration, but Mom said she watched for signs of frustration and said, "Last one!" ending by sharing a "story-snack." Sitting next to each other on the couch, Mom would tell Jordy a story about when he was little. Every time she said his name, she held a piece of snack near her eye level. When Jordy made eye contact, she placed the treat in his mouth. Soon his eyes lingered on Mom as she told the story. Mom had practiced holding his hand at the end of the story to keep contact as they ended with the special handshake they had developed.

Jordy had access to his screen time following their dyadic play. "He doesn't even seem addicted to that screen, now," she said incredulously. On two days, Jordy had anticipated "getting off" the electronics and there were no meltdowns. On another day, Jordy smiled when his brother Andrew walked into the living room with a pillow used to make a hiding surprise. Jordy looked at Mom and said, "Mom, look!" He stopped his screen time to play with Andrew. Mom had tears in her eyes as she described this. Dad smiled at her. "It touches your heart when you see Jordy 'want' to play with Andrew and come out of his shell!" I said. They agreed. It was exhausting to always be on guard, trying to prevent meltdowns and injury. There was more hope now and they were relaxing more.

Therapeutic note: Joint attention, the ability of two people to notice and communicate about a shared experience (e.g., regarding another person, pet, or object) is a developmental process that neurotypical children readily exhibit. As Jordy experienced the felt sense of safety and predictability in Theraplay, Mom was able to activate his social engagement system (Porges 2017) and practice the up- and downregulation associated with maintaining an optimal level of arousal (Lindaman & Booth 2010, p.110; Lindaman & Mäkelä 2018). Theraplay's interpersonal sensorimotor play addressed his multiple needs for regulation: emotionally, with positive affect and connection, and physically, via his proprioceptive and vestibular needs. They practiced joint attention discovering the smell of different kinds of lotion, and how many pillows they could balance on their heads as they sat together. Once Jordy's need for connection and regulation was addressed, he was able to initiate and generalize his own joint attention skills by cueing and commenting to Mom to notice Andrew's bid to play (Kasari *et al.* 2012).

Sessions 13, 14, 15, with Mom

With Mom as co-therapist leading the sessions, these addressed how Jordy increased his emotional intensity. Mom practiced clear directions, physical guidance, and calming. Jordy practiced Mom's directions for fast and slow wiggles in and out, hard and soft touch with lotion and hugs, and bilateral coordination challenges in "Simon says" (e.g., "Touch right hand to left knee and left hand to right toe!"). As Mom realized how much physical moving and jumping Jordy needed, and how helpful eye contact was to help him regulate, we wondered if music plus movement could help. What emerged was a Theraplay version of the polka activated by eye contact. When Jordy engaged with eye contact, Mom and I took turns counting and spinning him to the music—polka style: One...two...three... spin... One...two...three...spin. He loved it and did show increased calm and focus.

Session 16, parent session

Mom and Dad each saw progress when they were alone with Jordy. However, when together as a family, he still showed notable regulation problems. When not using his iPad, he was described as antsy, frequently spinning himself in circles until he either hurt himself or his parents had to sternly correct him. They reported their frustration and embarrassment when Jordy spun himself into a tower of baby toys at Walmart, knocking them over. Fortunately, Jordy was unhurt and the toys were not damaged. He responded with surprise and laughed. This precipitated a "pack-n-port" (Bundy-Myrow 2000) regulation plan called "Tuna mush" that entailed using the "three times rule" to progressively teach the task. Dad chose to practice this plan with me during the upcoming family sessions. Components were: "T" sign with hands to communicate "time to stop" when Dad said the word "tuna." Jordy would freeze in place. When Dad added the word "mush," Jordy learned to walk to Dad to get (and give) a big squeeze.

Sessions 17, 18, 19, with family, including baby brother Andrew

Dad led these sessions with my assistance so the family could experience Dad as a leader who could foster family fun. Through guided modeling and feedback, his skills had dramatically increased. Andrew sat in Mom's lap. Session 17 consisted of the following activities:

- Greeting song with scarf "Peek-a-boo", e.g., "Where, oh where, is our friend X?... Peek-a-boo!" as the scarf is removed; check-in counting teeth – Jordy helped.

- "You lookin' at me?"—sitting in a circle holding a blanket, each member took a turn making eye contact with another. Dad introduced the word "tuna," which meant "stop and look." The leader said, "One...two...three...tuna, look at me," and all raised the blanket. The receiver of eye contact said, "You lookin' at me?" All clapped.

- Tunnels: especially fun for Andrew as Dad, Jordy, and I raised the sheet for Andrew to crawl under to receive Mom's hug.

- Snack share: Dad fed Jordy, and Jordy shared with Andrew as Mom assisted.

- Good-bye song and group hug: as Jordy started to "wind up," Mom began to hum *Oh, My Jordy!* I asked Jordy if it was okay to sing his special Jordy song for the whole family. We did.

The need for Dad to provide additional structure for Jordy was practiced in games like "Red light/green light," which became "Tuna, go," split attention games like hot potato, and simultaneously listening for the word "tuna" to freeze a game. It was rewarding to hear Dad's confidence increase as he told me about using their secret code word at home and in public. The word "tuna" was paired with "freezing" and looking at Dad. The rewarding part was the word "mush"—when Jordy gave and received Dad's squeeze.

Session 20, getting ready to terminate

Jordy was more regulated and positive, as were Mom and Dad. A Theraplay party is a well-earned celebration, and we planned with Jordy's favorite activities, snacks, and beverage.

Session 21, party

Jordy had indicated his favorite activities were: hide and seek; dance, freeze, hug, using "Tuna mush"; blanket swing for each of the boys; balloon balance with little Andrew as the official balloon-holder; snack with "flying pretzels" passed along a long licorice rope; and *Oh, My Jordy!* The family rocked their boys in a big hug and we all sang.

Case outcome

Theraplay helped Jordy and his family members in different but complementary ways. Mom learned to continue her positive involvement when Jordy was frustrated, and to guide or remind him to breathe, calm, and "make a plan" to solve the problem. She felt proud of his efforts to succeed. Structure helped her with transitions so their schedule would work more smoothly. Theraplay coaching helped Dad support Mom's structure and the Theraplay process helped him to develop a strong alliance with his son. Jordy became comfortable letting his parents lead; they could have fun together and they helped him when he was upset or very excited. With Andrew, Jordy became gentler and more flexible. By feeling stable and supported on the home front, Jordy was better able to address peer relationships via "lunch bunch" and group counseling at school. In this case, his parents were able to support each other. However, as there is often significant stress on the marriages of couples with special needs children such as those on the autism spectrum, the Theraplay therapist can assist by anticipating changes in adult dynamics, supporting the couple via parent coaching, referring to local support groups, individual and marriage counseling, and social media groups such as Bright and Quirky.[2]

Conclusion

When a Theraplay therapist engages a child on the autism spectrum, they use the essential elements of Theraplay to connect with the "me" of autism and develop the "we" of dyadic relationships.

The case of Jordy, a seven-year-old boy at the moderate end of the autism spectrum, illustrates why Theraplay is an essential therapeutic experience for children on the autism spectrum and their families. Theraplay enables interpersonal experiences by way of attuned, multisensory, attachment-based play. The Theraplay therapist becomes the social translator who guides parents to understand both the world of autism and how to use the Theraplay dimensions of structure and nurture to increase behavioral regulation. Family Theraplay is critical to expand restricted interests, counter withdrawal, and increase the child's access to their caregivers as a resource for comfort, reassurance, and validation.

---

2   https://brightandquirky.com

References

Adamson, L. B., Bakerman, R., Deckner, D. F., & Nelson, P. B. (2012). Rating parent–child interactions: Joint engagements, communication dynamics, and shared topics in autism, down syndrome, and typical development. *Journal of Autism Development Disorder 42*, 2622–2635. https://doi.org/10.1007/s10803-012-1520-1

Aldred, C., Green, J., & Adams, C. (2004). A new social communication intervention for children with autism: Pilot randomized controlled treatment study suggesting effectiveness. *Journal of Child Psychology and Psychiatry 45*, 1420–1430. doi: 10.1111/j.1469-7610.2004.00848.x

APA (American Psychiatric Association). (2013). *Diagnostic and Statistical Manual of Mental Disorders* (5th edn). American Psychiatric Association.

Azoulay, D. (2000). Theraplay® with Physically Handicapped and Developmentally Delayed Children. In E. Munns (ed.) *Theraplay®: Innovations in Attachment-Enhancing Play Therapy* (pp.280–300). Jason-Aronson.

Badenoch, B. (2008). *Being a Brain-Wise Therapist: A Practical Guide to Interpersonal Neurobiology.* Norton.

Baldini, L. L., Parker, S. C., Nelson, B. W., & Siegel, D. J. (2014). The clinician as neuroarchitect: The importance of mindfulness and presence in clinical practice. *Clinical Social Work 43*, 218–227. https://doi.org/10.1007/s10615-014-0476-3

Booth, P., & Koller, T. J. (1998). Training Parents of Failure-to-Attach Children. In J. M. Briesmeister and C. E. Schaefer (eds) *Handbook of Parent Training: Training Parents as Co-Therapists for Children's Behavior Problems* (2nd edn) (pp.308–343). Wiley.

Bostrom, J. (1995). Fostering attachment in post-institutionalized adopted children using Group Theraplay. *The Theraplay Institute Newsletter*, Fall, 7–8.

Bottema-Beutel, K., Yoder, P., Woynaroski, T., & Sandbank, M. P. (2014). Targeted Interventions for Social Communication Symptoms in Preschoolers with Autism Spectrum Disorders. In F. R. Volkmar, S. J. Rogers, R. Paul, & K. A. Pelphrey (eds) *Handbook of Autism and Pervasive Developmental Disorders* (4th edn) (pp.788–812). John Wiley & Sons.

Bowlby, J. (1969). *Attachment and Loss, Vol. 1: Attachment.* Basic Books.

Bundy-Myrow, S. (2000). Group Theraplay for Children with Autism and Pervasive Developmental Disorder. In E. Munns (ed.) *Theraplay Innovations in Attachment-Enhancing Play Therapy* (pp.301–320). Jason Aronson.

Burns, D., with Burns, S. L. (no date). *Tools, Not Schools of Therapy* [eBook]. https://feelinggood.com/product/tools-not-schools-of-therapy

Center for Autism & Related Disorders. (2022). Autism Care Today honors Center for Autism and Related Disorders (CARD). www.centerforautism.com/resources/autism-care-today

Constantino, J. N., & Gruber, C. P. (2007). *Social Responsiveness Scale (SRS)*. Western Psychological Services.

Cooper, J. O., Heron, T. E., & Heward, W. L. (2007). *Applied Behavior Analysis* (2nd edn). Pearson Education.

Davidovitch, M., Slobodin, O., Weisskopf, M. G., & Rotem, R. S. (2020). Age-specific time trends in incidence rates of autism spectrum disorder following adaptation of DSM-5 and other ASD-related regulatory changes in Israel. *Autism Research* 13(11), 1893–1901. https://doi.org/10.1002/aur.2420

DesLauriers, A. M, & Carlson, C. F. (1969). *Your Child is Asleep—Early Infantile Autism: Etiology, Treatment, and Parental Influences.* Dorsey Press.

Durand, M. (2011). *Optimistic Parenting: Hope and Help for You and Your Challenging Child.* Brookes Publishing.

Franklin, J., Moore, E., Howard, A., Purvis, K., Cross, D., & Lindaman, S. (2007). An Evaluation of Theraplay Using a Sample of Children Diagnosed with Pervasive Developmental Disorder (PDD) or Mild to Moderate Autism. Poster presentation at the American Psychological Association Conference.

Frost, L., & Bondy, A. (2002). *The Picture Exchange Communication System: Training Manual.* Pyramid Educational Consultants.

Gutierrez, A., Fischer, A. J., Hale, M. N., Durocher, J. S., & Alessandri, M. (2013). Differential response patterns to the control condition between two procedures to assess social reinforcers for children with autism. *Behavioral Interventions* 28(4), 353–361. https://doi.org/10.1002/bin.1372

Hagopian, L. P., Long, E. S., & Rush, K. S. (2004). Preference assessment procedures for individuals with developmental disabilities. *Behavior Modification 26*, 668–677. https://doi.org/10.1177/0145445503259836

Hiles Howard, A. R., Lindaman, S., Copeland, R., & Cross, D. R. (2018). Theraplay impact on parents and children with autism spectrum disorder: Improvements in affect, joint attention, and social cooperation. *International Journal of Play Therapy 27*(1), 56–68. https://doi.org/10.1037/pla0000056

Hughes, D. (2011). *Attachment Focused Family Therapy Workbook.* W.W. Norton & Company.

Iacoboni, M. (2007). Face to face: The neural basis of social mirroring and empathy. *Psychiatric Annals 37*(4), 236–241. https://doi.org/10.3928/00485713-20070401-05

Iacoboni, M. (2009). Imitation, empathy, and mirror neurons. *Annual Review of Psychology 60*, 653–670. doi: 10.1146/annurev.psych.60.110707.163604

Iovino, L., Canniello, F., Simeoli, R., Gallucci, M., Benincasa, R., D'Elia, D., Hanley, G. P., & Cammilieri, A. P. (2022). A new adaptation of the Interview-Informed Synthesized Contingency Analyses (IISCA): The performance-based IISCA. *European Journal of Behavior Analysis 23*(2), 144–155. https://doi.org/10.1080/15021149.2022.2093596

Jernberg, A. M. (1984). Theraplay: Child therapy for attachment fostering. *Psychotherapy 21*(1), 39–47. https://doi.org/10.1037/h0087526

Jernberg, A. M., & Booth, P. B. (2001). *Theraplay: Helping Parents and Children Build Better Relationships Through Attachment Based Play.* Jossey-Bass Publishers.

Jernberg, A. M., Hurst, T., & Lyman, C. (1969). Here I Am. [16 mm film, available from The Theraplay Institute, 1224 W. Belmont Avenue, Chicago, IL 60657.]

Jernberg, A. M., Hurst, T., & Lyman, C. (1975). There He Goes. [16 mm film, available from The Theraplay Institute, 1224 W. Belmont Avenue, Chicago, IL 60657].

Jones, E. A., & Carr, E. G. (2004). Joint attention in children with autism: Theory and intervention. *Focus on Autism and Other Developmental Disabilities 19*, 13–26. https://doi.org/10.1177/10883576040190010301

Kasari, C., Gulsrud, A. C., Kwon, S., & Locke, J. (2010). Randomized controlled caregiver mediated joint engagement intervention for toddlers with autism. *Journal of Autism and Developmental Disorder 40*, 1045–1056. http://dx.doi.org/10.1007/s10803-010-0955-5

Kasari, C., Gulsrud, A., Freeman, S., Paparella, T., & Hellemann, G. (2012). Longitudinal follow-up of children with autism receiving targeted interventions on joint attention and play. *Journal of the American Academy of Child & Adolescent Psychiatry 51*(5), 487–495. http://dx.doi.org/10.1016/j.jaac.2012.02.019

Koegel, R. L., & Koegel, L. K. (2018). *Pivotal Response Treatment for Autism Spectrum Disorders* (2nd edn). Paul Brooks Publishing Co.

Lindaman, S., & Booth, P. (2010). Theraplay for Children with Autism Spectrum Disorders. In P. B. Booth & A. M. Jernberg (eds) *Theraplay: Helping Parents and Children Build Better Relationships Through Attachment-Based Play* (pp.301–358). John Wiley & Sons.

Lindaman, S., & Mäkelä, J. (2018). The Polyvagal Foundation of Theraplay Treatment: Combining Social Engagement, Play, and Nurture to Create Safety, Regulation, and Resilience. In S. W. Porges & D. Dana (eds) *Clinical Applications of the Polyvagal Theory: The Emergence of Polyvagal-Informed Therapies* (pp.227–247). W.W. Norton & Company.

Lindgren, S., & Doobay, A. (2011). *Evidence-Based Interventions for AUTISM Spectrum Disorders.* For the Iowa Department of Human Services by the Center for Disabilities and Development, University of Iowa Children's Hospital.

Lorenz, K. (1961). *King Solomon's Ring.* Translated by Marjorie Kerr Wilson. Methuen.

Lovaas, I. O., & Simmons, J. Q. (1969). Manipulation of self-destruction in three retarded children. *Journal of Applied Behavior Analysis 2*, 143–157. doi: 10.1901/jaba.1969.2-143

Mäkelä, J., & Vierikko, I. (2004). *From Heart to Heart: Interactive Therapy for Children in Care. Report on the Theraplay Project in SOS Children's Villages in Finland 2001–2004*. SOS Children's Village, Finland.

National Autism Center (2015). *Findings and Conclusions: National Standards Project, Phase 2*. National Autism Center.

NPDC (National Professional Development Center on Autism Spectrum Disorders). (no date). http://autismpdc.fpg.unc.edu/national-professional-development-center-autism-spectrum-disorder

NPDC (National Professional Development Center on Autism Spectrum Disorders). (2022). What are evidenced-based practices? https://autismpdc.fpg.unc.edu/evidence-based-practices

Oberman, L. M., Hubbard, E. M., McCleery, J. P., Altschuler, E. L., Ramachandran, V. S., & Pineda, J. A. (2005). EEG evidence for mirror neuron dysfunction in autism spectrum disorders. *Cognitive Brain Research 24*(2), 190–198. doi: 10.1016/j.cogbrainres.2005.01.014

Porges, S. W. (2011). *The Polyvagal Theory: Neurophysiological Foundations of Emotions, Attachment, Communication, and Self-Regulation*. W.W. Norton & Company.

Porges, S. W. (2015). Making the world safe for our children: Down-regulating defence and up-regulating social engagement to "optimise" the human experience. *Children Australia 40*, 114–123. doi: 10.1017/cha.2015.12

Porges, S. W. (2017). *The Pocket Guide to the Polyvagal Theory: The Transformative Power of Feeling Safe*. W.W. Norton & Company.

Reeve, C. (2021). Murdoch Program Library: A great tool for teaching life skills. Autism Classroom News & Resources. https://autismclassroomresources.com/murdoch-program-library-a-tool-for-teaching-life-skills

Ruble, L., McDuffie, A., King, A. S., & Lorenz, D. (2008). Caregiver responsiveness and social interaction behaviors of young children with autism. *Topics in Early Childhood Special Education 28*, 158–170. doi: 10.1177/0271121408323009

Rutter, M. (2007). Gene–Environment Interplay and Developmental Psychopathology. In A. S. Masten (ed.) *Multilevel Dynamics in Developmental Psychopathology: Pathways to the Future. The Minnesota Symposia on Child Psychology*, Vol. 34 (pp.1–26). Erlbaum.

Sandbank, M., Bottema-Beutel, K., Crowley, S., Cassidy, M., Dunham, K., Feldman, J. I., Crank, J., Albarran, S. A., Raj, S., Mahbub, P., & Woynaroski, T. G. (2020). Project AIM: Autism intervention meta-analysis for studies of young children. *Psychological Bulletin 146*(1), 1–29. doi: 10.1037/bul0000215

Schore, A. N. (2014). Early interpersonal neurobiological assessment of attachment and autistic spectrum disorders. *Frontiers in Psychology 5*, 1–13. doi: 10.3389/fpsyg.2014.01049

Schramm, R., with Miller, M. (2014). *The Seven Steps to Earning Instructional Control: A Program Guide for Developing Learner Cooperation with ABA and Verbal Behavior*. Pro-ABA.

Schreibman, L., Dawson, G., Stahmer, A. C., Landa, R., Rogers, S. J., McGee, G. G., Kasari, C., Ingersoll, B., Kaiser, A. P., Bruinsma, Y., McNerney, E., Wetherby, A., & Halladay, A. (2015). Naturalistic developmental behavioral interventions: Empirically validated treatments for autism spectrum disorder. *Journal of Autism and Developmental Disorders 45*, 2411–2428. http://dx.doi.org/10.1007/s10803-015-2407-8

Siegel, D. (2001). Toward an interpersonal neurobiology of the developing mind: Attachment relationships, "mindsight," and neural integration. *Infant Mental Health Journal 22*(1–2), 67–94. https://doi.org/10.1002/1097-0355(200101/04)22:1<67::AID-IMHJ3>3.0.CO;2-G

Siu, A. F. Y. (2009). Theraplay® in the Chinese world: An intervention program for Hong Kong children with behavior problems. *International Journal of Play Therapy 18*(1), 1–12. https://doi.org/10.1037/a0013979

Siu, A. F. Y. (2014). Effectiveness of group Theraplay® on enhancing social skills among children with developmental disabilities. *International Journal of Play Therapy 23*(4), 187–203. https://doi.org/10.1037/a0038158

Tamis-LeMonda, C. S., Bornstein, M. H., & Baumwell, L. (2001). Maternal responsiveness and children's achievement of language milestones. *Child Development 72*(3), 748–767. www.jstor.org/stable/1132453

Tronick, E., & Beeghly, M. (2011). Infants' meaning-making and the development of mental health problems. *American Psychologist 66*(2), 107–119. doi: 10.1037/a0021631

van Kessel, R., Roman-Urrestarazu, A., Ruigrok, A., Holt, R., Commers, M., Hoekstra, R. A., Czabanowska, K., Brayne, C., & Baron, S. (2019). Autism and family involvement in the right to education in the EU: Policy mapping in the Netherlands, Belgium, and Germany. *Molecular Autism 10*(43). doi: 10.1186/s13229-019-0297-x

Wang, A. T., Lee, S. S., Sigman, M., & Dapretto, M. (2007). Reading affect in the face and voice: Neural correlates of interpreting communicative intent in children and adolescents with autism spectrum disorders. *Archives of General Psychiatry 64*(6), 698–708. doi: 10.1001/archpsyc.64.6.698

Wetherby, A. M., & Woods, J. J. (2006). Early social interaction project for children with autism spectrum disorders beginning in the second year of life: A preliminary study. *Topics in Early Childhood Special Education 26*(2), 67–82. http://dx.doi.org/10.1177/02711214060260020201

Wettig, H. H. G., Coleman, A. R., & Geider, F. J. (2011). Evaluating the effectiveness of Theraplay® in treating shy, socially withdrawn children. *International Journal of Play Therapy 20*(1), 26–37. https://doi.org/10.1037/a0022666

Wheeler, A. J., Miller, R. A., Springer, B. M., Pittard, N. C., Phillips, J. F., & Myers, A. M. (1997). *Murdoch Center Program Library* (3rd edn). Murdoch Center Foundation.

Winnicott, D. W. (1965). *The Maturational Processes and the Facilitating Environment: Studies in the Theory of Emotional Development*. Hogarth Press.

Appendix 1

Task Analysis

Any task can be mapped out on a worksheet like these. For caregivers, this gives a clear structure to the process of teaching. For those who are working with in-home therapists and teachers on the tasks, it increases the likelihood that everyone will do the task in same way each time. The multiple columns allow for tracking success and improvement over time by showing a decrease in the amount or level of prompting needed. Some children enjoy seeing this progress and also find it motivating.

Task analysis: Laundry

Task steps	Level of prompting	Level of prompting	Level of prompting	Level of prompting
Put the lid down to access the dial	Independent Gestural prompt Verbal prompt Partial physical Full physical	Independent Gestural prompt Verbal prompt Partial physical Full physical	Independent Gestural prompt Verbal prompt Partial physical Full physical	Independent Gestural prompt Verbal prompt Partial physical Full physical
Turn dial to setting	Independent Gestural prompt Verbal prompt Partial physical Full physical	Independent Gestural prompt Verbal prompt Partial physical Full physical	Independent Gestural prompt Verbal prompt Partial physical Full physical	Independent Gestural prompt Verbal prompt Partial physical Full physical
Turn on the washer: pull out the dial to start the flow of water	Independent Gestural prompt Verbal prompt Partial physical Full physical	Independent Gestural prompt Verbal prompt Partial physical Full physical	Independent Gestural prompt Verbal prompt Partial physical Full physical	Independent Gestural prompt Verbal prompt Partial physical Full physical
Set the lid back slightly, avoiding turning off the water	Independent Gestural prompt Verbal prompt Partial physical Full physical	Independent Gestural prompt Verbal prompt Partial physical Full physical	Independent Gestural prompt Verbal prompt Partial physical Full physical	Independent Gestural prompt Verbal prompt Partial physical Full physical

Measure out detergent	Independent Gestural prompt Verbal prompt Partial physical Full physical	Independent Gestural prompt Verbal prompt Partial physical Full physical	Independent Gestural prompt Verbal prompt Partial physical Full physical	Independent Gestural prompt Verbal prompt Partial physical Full physical	Independent Gestural prompt Verbal prompt Partial physical Full physical
Pour detergent into the water	Independent Gestural prompt Verbal prompt Partial physical Full physical	Independent Gestural prompt Verbal prompt Partial physical Full physical	Independent Gestural prompt Verbal prompt Partial physical Full physical	Independent Gestural prompt Verbal prompt Partial physical Full physical	Independent Gestural prompt Verbal prompt Partial physical Full physical
Put clothes into the washer	Independent Gestural prompt Verbal prompt Partial physical Full physical	Independent Gestural prompt Verbal prompt Partial physical Full physical	Independent Gestural prompt Verbal prompt Partial physical Full physical	Independent Gestural prompt Verbal prompt Partial physical Full physical	Independent Gestural prompt Verbal prompt Partial physical Full physical
Close the lid	Independent Gestural prompt Verbal prompt Partial physical Full physical	Independent Gestural prompt Verbal prompt Partial physical Full physical	Independent Gestural prompt Verbal prompt Partial physical Full physical	Independent Gestural prompt Verbal prompt Partial physical Full physical	Independent Gestural prompt Verbal prompt Partial physical Full physical

Task analysis: Transfer from washer to drier

Task steps	Level of prompting	Level of prompting	Level of prompting	Level of prompting
Open the drier door and take out any clothes	Independent Gestural prompt Verbal prompt Partial physical Full physical	Independent Gestural prompt Verbal prompt Partial physical Full physical	Independent Gestural prompt Verbal prompt Partial physical Full physical	Independent Gestural prompt Verbal prompt Partial physical Full physical
Lift the lid of the washer to access the wet clothes	Independent Gestural prompt Verbal prompt Partial physical Full physical	Independent Gestural prompt Verbal prompt Partial physical Full physical	Independent Gestural prompt Verbal prompt Partial physical Full physical	Independent Gestural prompt Verbal prompt Partial physical Full physical
Take clothes out and put them into the drier	Independent Gestural prompt Verbal prompt Partial physical Full physical	Independent Gestural prompt Verbal prompt Partial physical Full physical	Independent Gestural prompt Verbal prompt Partial physical Full physical	Independent Gestural prompt Verbal prompt Partial physical Full physical
Close the drier door	Independent Gestural prompt Verbal prompt Partial physical Full physical	Independent Gestural prompt Verbal prompt Partial physical Full physical	Independent Gestural prompt Verbal prompt Partial physical Full physical	Independent Gestural prompt Verbal prompt Partial physical Full physical

Push the power button to turn on the drier	Independent Gestural prompt Verbal prompt Partial physical Full physical	Independent Gestural prompt Verbal prompt Partial physical Full physical	Independent Gestural prompt Verbal prompt Partial physical Full physical	Independent Gestural prompt Verbal prompt Partial physical Full physical
Set the button on "Regular"	Independent Gestural prompt Verbal prompt Partial physical Full physical	Independent Gestural prompt Verbal prompt Partial physical Full physical	Independent Gestural prompt Verbal prompt Partial physical Full physical	Independent Gestural prompt Verbal prompt Partial physical Full physical
Completely close the lid	Independent Gestural prompt Verbal prompt Partial physical Full physical	Independent Gestural prompt Verbal prompt Partial physical Full physical	Independent Gestural prompt Verbal prompt Partial physical Full physical	Independent Gestural prompt Verbal prompt Partial physical Full physical
Push "Start"	Independent Gestural prompt Verbal prompt Partial physical Full physical	Independent Gestural prompt Verbal prompt Partial physical Full physical	Independent Gestural prompt Verbal prompt Partial physical Full physical	Independent Gestural prompt Verbal prompt Partial physical Full physical

Joint Attention Observational Coding System Embedded with Marschak Interaction Methods (MIM) Analysis Form for Children on the Autism Spectrum

Structure (dyad observation)

1. Caregiver provides structure and directions.

2. Child accepts structure and directions or is defiant, insisting on doing things his/her own way.

3. Caregiver's efforts to structure and organize help regulate the child.

4. What role does the caregiver take?

   a. Caregiver in peer or child role.

   b. Caregiver unable to set limits.

   c. Caregiver turns authority over to child.

   d. Caregiver in teacher role (pedantic, rigid, focused only on task at hand).

Observations of verbal and non-verbal interactions that support conclusions about child and structure:

Caregiver 1 and structure:

Caregiver 2 and structure:

Engagement (dyad observation)

1. Caregiver able to engage the child and explain how they engage the child.

2. Child's response to caregiver's attempts to engage.

3. Caregiver responds empathically to the child.

4. Caregiver and child are physically and affectively in tune with each other.

5. Caregiver matches level of stimulation to child's ability to tolerate it.

6. The two are having fun together.

Observations of verbal and non-verbal interactions that support conclusions about child and engagement:

Caregiver 1 and engagement:

Caregiver 2 and engagement:

Joint attention observational coding system for child (Part 1)

Instruction: after a warm-up period (1–2 minutes), check "Y" when a behavior is observed, regardless of the frequency of the behavior, with a 30-second interval. Choose two activities from three engagement activities and stop coding at three minutes respectively. Add up the total number of "Y." Note quality of a behavior (e.g., most frequent behavior) in the observational summary.

Task: Squeaky animals (seconds)	Non-verbal affect		Verbal affect		Initiation		Responses		Eye gaze		Mirroring		Total # of Y
0–30	Y	N	Y	N	Y	N	Y	N	Y	N	Y	N	
31–60	Y	N	Y	N	Y	N	Y	N	Y	N	Y	N	
61–90	Y	N	Y	N	Y	N	Y	N	Y	N	Y	N	
91–120	Y	N	Y	N	Y	N	Y	N	Y	N	Y	N	
121–150	Y	N	Y	N	Y	N	Y	N	Y	N	Y	N	
151–180	Y	N	Y	N	Y	N	Y	N	Y	N	Y	N	
3 minutes	# of Y:		# of Y:		# of Y:		# of Y:		# of Y:		# of Y:		# of Y:
Observational summary													

Task: Familiar games (seconds)	Non-verbal affect		Verbal affect		Initiation		Responses		Eye gaze		Mirroring		Total # of Y
0–30	Y	N	Y	N	Y	N	Y	N	Y	N	Y	N	
31–60	Y	N	Y	N	Y	N	Y	N	Y	N	Y	N	
61–90	Y	N	Y	N	Y	N	Y	N	Y	N	Y	N	
91–120	Y	N	Y	N	Y	N	Y	N	Y	N	Y	N	
121–150	Y	N	Y	N	Y	N	Y	N	Y	N	Y	N	
151–180	Y	N	Y	N	Y	N	Y	N	Y	N	Y	N	
3 minutes	# of Y:		# of Y:		# of Y:		# of Y:		# of Y:		# of Y:		# of Y:
Observational summary													

Task: Putting hats on each other (seconds)	Non-verbal affect		Verbal affect		Initiation		Responses		Eye gaze		Mirroring		Total # of Y
0–30	Y	N	Y	N	Y	N	Y	N	Y	N	Y	N	
31–60	Y	N	Y	N	Y	N	Y	N	Y	N	Y	N	
61–90	Y	N	Y	N	Y	N	Y	N	Y	N	Y	N	
91–120	Y	N	Y	N	Y	N	Y	N	Y	N	Y	N	
121–150	Y	N	Y	N	Y	N	Y	N	Y	N	Y	N	
151–180	Y	N	Y	N	Y	N	Y	N	Y	N	Y	N	
3 minutes	# of Y:		# of Y:		# of Y:		# of Y:		# of Y:		# of Y:		# of Y:
Observational summary													

Nurture

1. Caregiver provides nurturing contact (touch, physical contact, caregiving).

2. Child accepts nurturing contact.

3. Caregiver asks child to take care of him/her.

4. Caregiver recognizes and acts on child's need for help in calming/ having stress reduced.

5. Child accepts parental help for calming/stress reduction.

6. Child is able to soothe self.

Joint attention observational coding system for child (Part 2)

Instruction: Begin after the caregiver and child take snacks out of the envelope. Check "Y" when a behavior is observed, regardless of the frequency of the behavior, with a 30-second interval. Stop at one minute and add up the total number of "Y." Note quality of a behavior (e.g., most frequent behavior) in the observational summary.

Task: Feeding (seconds)	Non-verbal affect		Verbal affect		Initiation		Responses		Eye gaze		Mirroring		Total # of Y
0–30	Y	N	Y	N	Y	N	Y	N	Y	N	Y	N	
31–60	Y	N	Y	N	Y	N	Y	N	Y	N	Y	N	
1 minute	# of Y:		# of Y:		# of Y:		# of Y:		# of Y:		# of Y:		# of Y:
Observational summary													

Leave the room task

1. Caregiver prepares child for separation.

   Note: Describe child's behavior during separation and at reunion.

   Caregiver tells child about when child came to live with caregiver (if adopted or in foster care). Alternatively, caregiver tells child about when child was an infant (if a birth child).

2. Nature of story.

3. Reflection about caregiver's/child's feelings.

4. Child's response.

5. Caregiver attunement to child's response.

Observations of verbal and non-verbal interacts that support conclusions about child and nurture:

Caregiver 1 and nurture:

Caregiver 2 and nurture:

Challenge

1. Activities chosen by the caregiver are developmentally appropriate.

2. Child responds to the task.

3. Caregiver makes mastery appealing.

4. Child is able to focus and concentrate.

5. Child is able to handle frustration.

6. Caregiver helps child handle frustration.

Observations of verbal and non-verbal interactions that support conclusions about:

Child and challenge: Activity 1, caregiver and child both take eight blocks. Caregiver builds a structure and asks the child to "build one just like mine." Or Activity 2, caregiver draws a picture with pen on paper and asks child to "draw one just like mine."

Caregiver 1 and challenge:

Caregiver 2 and challenge:

Joint attention observational coding system for child (Part 3)

Instruction: Begin coding after the caregiver and child pull out the blocks from the envelope. Check "Y" when a behavior is observed, regardless of the frequency of the behavior, with a 30-second interval. Stop at three minutes and add up the total number of "Y." Note quality of a behavior (e.g., most frequent behavior) in the observational summary.

Task: Blocks (seconds)	Non-verbal affect		Verbal affect		Initiation		Responses		Eye gaze		Mirroring		Total # of Y
0–30	Y	N	Y	N	Y	N	Y	N	Y	N	Y	N	
31–60	Y	N	Y	N	Y	N	Y	N	Y	N	Y	N	
61–90	Y	N	Y	N	Y	N	Y	N	Y	N	Y	N	
91–120	Y	N	Y	N	Y	N	Y	N	Y	N	Y	N	
121–150	Y	N	Y	N	Y	N	Y	N	Y	N	Y	N	
151–180	Y	N	Y	N	Y	N	Y	N	Y	N	Y	N	
3 minutes	# of Y:		# of Y:		# of Y:		# of Y:		# of Y:		# of Y:		# of Y:
Observational summary													

Total baseline score of child's joint attention capacities:

Child's most frequent joint attention behavior and its score:

Child's least frequent joint attention behavior and its score:

Subject Index

Sub-headings in *italics* indicate tables.

Author Index